JOYFUL BALANCE

How to Achieve Success and Happiness, in Work, Life, and Beyond

Nash Narasimhan Tupil

Clever Fox® PUBLISHING
Chennai • Bangalore

I have known Nash for almost three decades as a colleague, and as someone I have been in touch with through his own journey in life- rediscovering himself and always finding a new balance in life. Besides, being a successful professional, he became an avid writer, a teacher, a biker, a coach and there is more ahead. This book very much reflects his own learnings and would help others in finding their own path.

The book urges all to judge success by looking inward - asking what brings me contentment, what aligns with my values and passions, how have I grown compared to my own past self? Rather than seeking validation through others, Nash advocates for regular self-reflection, mindful observation, and adjusting life plans with our own unique preferences. Ultimately, the most important measure is personal satisfaction with the journey taken and positive impact left.

Who will benefit from this book? Anyone seeking to thrive, not just survive in an uncertain world: the young grappling with career choices, mid-stage leaders struggling with balance, or seasoned executives wondering about their legacy and where from here? Joyful Balance is both a compass and a map to help you recalibrate life—towards purpose and happiness.

Som Mittal

Former President & Chairman, NASSCOM

AUTHOR'S NOTE

When I joined IT industry 3 decades back, Som was our MD and I was his admirer. He had the habit of having lunch with fresh joiners. As a rookie professional, it was a dream come true, when I had lunch with him one day. Never in my wildest dreams, I would have imagined he would write the foreword for my book one day. Credit to Som, who stayed in touch and was kind enough to give this testimonial. Despite Som requiring no introduction, as his admirer, I need to mention about him a bit.

Som Mittal is Current Chairman, Patients for Patient Safety Foundation, Former Chairman & President, NASSCOM, Former Senior Vice President of HP Services for Asia-Pacific and Japan, Former CEO, Wipro PC, Server and Services division, Former MD, Digital Equipment & Compaq India, Distinguished Alumnus: IIT Kanpur, IIM Ahmedabad MBA, WITSA Lifetime Achievement Award, Rotary International Business Leader of the Year and Dataquest IT Person of the Year. He continues to be an inspiration for many in Indian IT industry.

TESTIMONIALS

From Corporate Leaders

Som Mittal, Former President & Chairman, NASSCOM, Ex-SVP HP Services Asia Pac, Ex-MD, Digital & Compaq India

Joyful Balance is *both a compass and a map* to help you recalibrate life, towards purpose and happiness. Nash offers a practical guide to rethink success, avoid burnout, and cultivate fulfilment. The young grappling with career choices, mid-stage leaders struggling with balance, or seasoned executives wondering about their legacy, all will benefit from this book.

Rajiv Srivastava, CEO & Co-Founder Coreops.AI. Ex Global MD & CEO Redington Ltd. Ex MD HP India Pvt ltd

Nash's book is a gentle yet **powerful reminder that success without inner alignment is incomplete**. He combines lived experience with actionable insight to help readers pursue achievement without losing balance - something that resonates deeply with me. In a world that celebrates speed, scale and visible success, this work brings us back to clarity, conscious living, and sustained equilibrium. It is a thoughtful guide for professionals, entrepreneurs and leaders seeking durable success anchored in purpose and well-being.

Ganesh Lakshminarayanan, MD & CEO, Tata Communications

I have known Nash for many years as a friend, sharing common interests in corporate life, religion, and Tamil. Joyful Balance, his book reflects Nash's sincerity and clarity through simple, practical frameworks, notably his structured view of life across six dimensions of Health, Happiness, Career, Care, Family, and Finance. *Joyful Balance is not theory; it is lived experience.* It comes from someone who has achieved, stumbled, learned, and rebuilt with clarity. If you are ambitious yet searching for deeper fulfilment, this book will feel honest, practical, and reassuring, **like a conversation with a trusted friend.**

Ketan Patel, President - Personal Systems, HP Inc.

Nash doesn't theorize, he mirrors reality. Mid-career in tech, I've watched brilliant colleagues hit peak titles, collect the BMW and the corner office, yet feel hollow inside — and quietly wondered if I was next. Chapter 1 felt like Nash had read my diary. His 6P framework isn't a concept; it's a compass I now live by. Success and happiness aren't rivals — they're partners. This book is that rare wake-up call.

Romal Shetty, CEO Deloitte South Asia

Joyful Balance is a thoughtful and deeply practical guide to redefining success in today's demanding world. Drawing from lived experience, *Nash blends wisdom, humility, and actionable frameworks*—like his powerful $(HCF)^2$ model—to demonstrate that achievement and happiness are not trade-offs, but partners.

By emphasising meta-skills that endure beyond titles and trends, this book reminds us that true leadership begins with balance—within ourselves and across the many dimensions of our lives.

Tian Chong Ng, CEO Singtel Singapore, Ex- MD HP Asia Pacific

This book is a powerful *reminder that success and happiness are not opposing forces*. Nash's insights, stories, and tools make the path to balance feel achievable, no matter where you are in your career or life journey. A refreshing and empowering read.

Kash Rangan, Ex-MD and Co-Head of Technology, Media & Telecom BU, Goldman Sachs

In 'Joyful Balance' Nash provides a very useful framework for managing work and life whereby they don't just co-exist but thrive synergistically. By being intentional, it is possible for one to nurture life's inspiring passions and relationships while pursuing one's corporate dreams.

Arun Kottolli, Ex- VP & Global CTO, JP Morgan Chase & Co

What makes this book so timely is how squarely it speaks to today's always-on, high-stakes professional reality. Whether you are leading teams, navigating a mid-career moment, or just trying to hold it all together, Nash's reflections on purpose and balance land with rare depth. *This is not a book you read and shelve, it stays*, gently shaping the quieter, wiser choices long after you have turned the last page.

Praveen Kutty, MD & CEO, DCB bank, India

Joyful Balance is a deeply insightful book drawing on practical personal experiences of Nash. It is lucid, succinct, and relatable. It is a book that *leaves you reflecting on your own purpose, long after you finished the last page.*

L Sridhar, Founder and Partner Sridhar & Brito, Visiting Faculty IIM, Bangalore

A small book, well written, lucid, easy to read, and full of meaningful substance. The book covers multiple perspectives like family values, work ethics, spirituality, seva and service. His ability to look at life with positivity and hope, treating challenging situations as God given opportunities to learn and grow comes out in this book. Nash has in his DNA the ability to write, communicate, share and motivate others, all life enhancing values, he meticulously gathered from an illustrious family background. *I would recommend all youngsters to read and gain insightful inspiration.*

Prad Mohanty, Global Business Head - Aerospace & Defence, Tata Consultancy Services

This book is a masterclass in authenticity and a must-read for anyone who wants to achieve great things while staying true to themselves. Nash is that rare kind of leader who is just as comfortable navigating a boardroom strategy, mentoring the next generation in a classroom, or riding his motorcycle through icy mountain passes living his "Portfolio life" every day. In Joyful Balance, he provides a powerful, actionable blueprint for anyone feeling the weight of the corporate grind, proving that reaching the top doesn't have to mean sacrificing your health, your family, or your inner spark.

GSS Srikanth, Ex-CEO, CSM Software (Solize India) Pvt Ltd

I have seen the sincerity and commitment Nash brings to everything he does. In his book, instead of telling readers what they must do, shares what he has learned, through real situations, real challenges, and real choices. The result is a set of reflections that feel relatable, practical, and genuinely achievable for the reader. Anyone navigating, a professional career, balancing ambition, responsibility, and personal life, will find something of value in these pages. *It is an honest, grounded read* that stays with you long after you have finished it.

Hideo Ohta, Ex-VP & Asia Pacific & Japan Head of HP Technology Services

Nash is a rare leader who understands how to think globally while staying connected to his roots. In Joyful Balance, he shares *thirty years of business experience in a useful way to help achieve long-term success.* Nash shows that **working too hard** and feeling burned out **is not necessary** for success. Being balanced and aligned is what really matters. If you want to choose both your career and your well-being, this book is a helpful guide for you.

Michelle Weiss, Ex-VP and Global Marketing head, Hewlett Packard Enterprise

This book provides a guide to life for those early in their career and those in mid-career. Drawing from his real-life experience as a burnt-out workaholic Nash goes on a journey and realizes that happiness breeds success and not the other way around. His book **offers practical tools** to *help anyone who needs to rebalance and recharge*. He has wisdom in abundance and an incomparable joie de vivre.

Gianluigi Redolfini, Ex- VP & Global Marketing head, Health Systems, Philips NV

Nash is a Born-Gentleman. He has an authentic ability to listen, to understand people beyond their roles, and to lead with humanity without ever compromising on results. Teams trusted and loved him not because of his title, but because of who he is and how he treats others. The book Joyful Balance is a natural extension of his personality. Nash shows that *high performance and personal fulfilment are not opposing forces*, **but complementary ones**. In a world that often rewards speed and scale, Nash reminds us that the **most enduring success** is *built on balance, purpose, and genuine care for people.*

Salil Punoose, CEO/CXO Coach, Ex-Director Unilever (Egypt), Ex-Chairman and MD Bestfoods India

Joyful Balance as a theme struck a chord in me. The book has high credibility because most of the concepts and thoughts were backed up by personal career examples of the author. The importance of spirituality in leading a balanced and meaningful life was unexpected in such a book, but so appropriate. I found the *book very easy to read and enjoy*. It was the right length; more important it was very logically structured in terms of flow. **I highly recommend this book** to all who face the issue of imbalance in their work life balance.

From non-corporate leaders

Prof Asit K Barma, Ph.D., Director, Bharathidasan Institute of Mgmt, Trichy

Nash's "Gully to Global" is a particularly compelling story, which traces his rise from modest beginnings to global executive leadership and candidly acknowledges the emotional costs of unchecked ambition. Unlike purely academic self-help texts, Joyful Balance stands out for its lived authenticity. The book blends memoir, self-help, and leadership philosophy, making it both relatable and actionable. Structured around six core forces—purpose, passion, potential, planning, people, and persistence—the narrative challenges common myths about work-life balance and the belief that happiness must wait until success is achieved. *This book serves as both a compass and a mirror, encouraging professionals to redefine success on their own terms and pursue their goals without sacrificing their inner well-being.*

Avinash Ananda, World's Leading Leadership & Happiness Coach, Co-creator, Meta Mind Alignment

Nash has presented a thoughtful and practical guide to creating a life of joyful balance. Drawing from his own life journey, he beautifully brings to life the Meta Mind principles into a clear and relatable roadmap for joyful living through his insightful life experiences and reflections, articulated in such an authentic and relatable style. The result is *a book that is both inspiring and actionable for anyone seeking success with balance and happiness.*

Ganesh Krishnamurthy, Founder: A Mindfulness Project (Auroville), Well-being & Transformation UnCoach

Narasimhan has poured his personal experience from his heart, weaving stories that are insightful and practical, to inspire both the young and the old, while exploring ideas on how one can lead a meaningful and happy life, while still balancing a number of categories of responsibilities, leading to coherence and authenticity, and in the process allowing individuals to **realise their highest human potential**. Hope you find it as interesting, as I did.

Sai Chandrashekar, Executive Director Operations, Agastya International Foundation

Joyful balance is a joy to read and practical. Unlike many other authors who share theoretical constructs, Nash has used his life experiences to build a case for joyful living. It does not feel like one is reading a book but feels more like having a conversation with Nash. He is nudging his readers to apply the learnings through worksheets so that readers can experience what he has. I would strongly recommend this for readers of all age groups.

Balaji Devanathan, Founder, Red Panda Adventures, Motorcycle adventure company

Nash was a co-rider in three of our adventure motorcycle expeditions. In 2021 to Darjeeling and Tawang. In 2025 to

Umling-La, the world's highest motorable pass in Ladakh. He signed up for these trips, at an age when most prefer comfort over challenge. High altitude, steep broken roads and biting cold were far outside his comfort zone. Yet he took these up as a challenge. He is enthusiastic, sincere and has clarity of purpose to show up every day. Even after many falls that injured and shook him, he chose to get back on the saddle the next morning. *Joyful Balance reflects that inner journey, of a resilient man, who has faced burnout and rebuilt himself quietly in his career and life.* This book will be useful for professionals seeking **sustained success without losing themselves along the way**.

Dr. K. Kamala, MD, Fellow of the International College of Surgeons (FICS), Ex-president, FOGSI

In this beautiful book, Nash Narasimhan, a global leader in e-commerce with passion for music, photography, teaching, trekking and motorbiking shares pearls of wisdom from his life. Starting from a modest job, he climbed great heights in his career. Despite his busy schedule, he found the time to keep all his above passions. His reflections show true happiness lies not in just reaching great career heights, but in returning home each day to family life filled with joy. *It's medically proven, balancing work tensions with joyful passions in this way, goes a long way in reducing hypertension, diabetes, premature aging and depression.*

T L Raghavan, Karnataka Shree awardee, Eminent Rotarian and author of over a dozen books.

A well written book, which will be useful *as a handbook not only on career but beyond in life.* Nash Narasimhan's advice to those in busy careers, to rest on one's oars and enjoy having a look around things, beyond their career is well articulated. Such diversions will not impinge on one's career output but help in bettering one's career. He is a living proof. He is more than a 'bathroom singer' and has passions for bike riding and photography with a beneficial footfall of well written blogs on his travels. Very happy he has imbibed the language and way of expression from his late father, a well-known sportswriter, whom I had the good fortune to know since my childhood.

Tanmay Dubey, Bestselling Author, Founder (Author Coaching Academy) & Ironman Triathlete

Most self-help books try to sell you success. Nash instead teaches you how to prevent success from stealing your happiness with his own examples. Nash is an energetic person and with almost childlike enthusiasm. He has curated this book into something that feels *less like advice and more like a life conversation with a trusted mentor*, narrate his life lessons with humility, warmth, and clarity. The section on meta-skills required for the future in the age of AI is particularly relevant for young professionals. Nash's giver's mindset, his belief in karma, integrity, and the power of doing good without expectation is not preachy; it is experiential. It is rare to find a corporate leader writing with this level of emotional honesty. I strongly believe Joyful Balance will **help many professionals design a life where success and happiness walk together.**

PART 1

THE CONTEXT FOR THIS BOOK

Chapter 1

THE MORNING I DIDN'T WANT TO GO TO WORK

Why this book?

It was a bright Monday morning in June 2014. At the time, I was serving as the APJ CMO (Asia Pacific & Japan, Chief Marketing Officer) for a multi-billion-dollar global IT company. By all outward measures, I had "made it." Yet that morning, I didn't feel like going to the office. In fact, I didn't feel like working at all. For the first time in my professional life, I felt a complete loss of meaning in what I was doing.

I shared this with my wife, Priya. She was concerned, but not entirely surprised. For nearly two decades, she had known me as an energetic, optimistic person—someone who loved going to work, thrived on achieving sales targets quarter after quarter, and inspired his team, earning recognition from his leaders as a model employee.

Priya respected me a lot, as a self-made individual. I come from a simple middle-class Indian family. Till I was 15 years, we lived in a joint family, which housed three generations from my paternal grandparents to my siblings. Later we sold the house and moved to smaller 2-bedroom apartment. A few months before my 12th standard board exams, my paternal grandparents came to our apartment and opted to stay with us for short period. My room was occupied by them and I was using the balcony and dining table for my studies and the hall to sleep at night.

But as a teenager, I had huge dreams and aspirations. To be someone successful, holding a good role in a big company, have a nice family, travel the world, live in a nice house, have a nice car. Responsibility came at an early age. I got married by 28, lost my father in a road accident when I was 30, took complete care of my mother after that and had my first daughter when I was 31 years. At 31 years I was the primary bread winner of my household, taking care of 3 generations, along with country P&L management role in a big IT MNC. By God's grace, and my hard work, I achieved most of what a middle-class person dreams of: stable job in a big company, nice family, nice house, nice car and chance to travel the world. All with my integrity and value systems intact. I am grateful.

However, over the last few months, my wife Priya had also watched me change. Each evening when I returned from the office, she noticed I was more drained than ever. The spark in my eyes, —the one that used to light up when I spoke about my work, my team, or my company—was gone. That morning, when I told her I didn't feel like going to work, her first question was whether I had a fever or a headache. I said no. Physically, I was fine. Mentally, I was not.

Priya was alarmed. In 18 years of marriage, she had never heard me say such words. What worried her even more was that my disinterest in work seemed to spill into other areas of life. I no longer asked for my favourite food. In fact, a special dish cooked by her, which I used to love a lot, did not enthuse me anymore. We loved holidays as a family, now I felt quite exhausted to even think about that. We loved to go to the movies as family with children, which did not interest me anymore. I used to play my favourite songs on my Hi-Fi system, even that failed to excite me. It wasn't just work I was withdrawing from—it was life itself.

Sadly, I had no hobbies too. For almost 20+ years, work and work-related travel was everything for me. As a sales professional, how my recent quarter closed and how the business looked in the future mattered a lot. I worked in matrixed organizations, where I had three different managers, I was accountable for my results. Some bosses were quite difficult. Similarly, my team, had multiple managers to work with. With reduced budgets, different expectations from different managers and push for incessant business growth, my team and I felt a lot of work pressure. So, a good or bad quarter in sales, could be a big thing for us.

My social circle was limited to my immediate family and few close friends. I did not have a hobby or social activities which gave me a sense of purpose and joy, beyond my business. Later I realized, how critical this is for a successful life.

This was burnout due to extreme work-related stress. I refused to see that. I thought this will go away in a few weeks, when a new quarter starts in sales. Priya urged me to see a doctor. I was postponing the trip to the doctor indefinitely. Eventually, this reached a stage, where I took the day off and went for a checkup in one of the reputed hospitals in the city. I went for a complete body check-up. Thankfully, all my reports showed my physical parameters were normal. But when the doctor began asking more profound questions about my work and life, it was difficult. He advised me to see a psychiatrist, who is qualified medical doctor (MD) specializing in mental health.

In our society, unlike physical illness, mental illness has social stigma attached to it. Only very recently, many people are coming out in the open with their struggles and seeking help. Frankly I was embarrassed about going to meet a psychiatrist. I eventually scheduled an appointment and met a psychiatrist for the first time in my life. When he asked me a few good questions, even talking about the problem to the doctor did not feel good for me. Priya had to chip in and explain. I was exhausted, disengaged, and showing clear signs of burnout. He confirmed, I was dealing with burnout and mild depression. He prescribed some medication, scheduled a follow-up, and strongly recommended I take at least a two-week break from work. And if it does not get better, quit my job and do different things in life.

It was a shock—for me, and for Priya. How had I reached this point? How did someone who had been a top performer, a high-flying executive managing multi-geo responsibilities, suddenly lose all joy in both work and life?

That moment marked the lowest point in my journey. But it was also the turning point. What followed was a slow, deliberate, and deeply transformative path—a journey that led me to what I now call Joyful Balance: the ability to achieve both success and happiness in work, life, and beyond.

And that is what this book is all about.

Chapter 2

WHEN SUCCESS STARTS FEELING EMPTY

Who is this book for?

I have spent over three decades in corporate life, working alongside some of the brightest minds and most accomplished leaders. Over the years, I have seen hundreds of high-profile executives rise to success. But I've also seen many who began their careers with immense promise only to lose their spark later in life. They struggled to sustain their energy, enthusiasm, and momentum. And often, their personal lives beyond work were far from fulfilling.

At the same time, I noticed a smaller group—a band of professionals who seemed different. They not only sustained their success at work but also radiated happiness in their personal lives. I often asked myself: What set them apart? Why can't I be like them? What is their secret to lasting success and happiness?

Driven by these questions, I began studying and modelling their behaviours. By God's grace, I found my own way—transforming from a state of breakdown to a breakthrough. Looking back, I often wish I had discovered these insights earlier. If I had known these principles sooner, I could have avoided the lowest points in my journey. I would have transitioned more smoothly from one role to the next, while also acing other aspects of life—health, family, and finance—with joy and balance.

And that's when it struck me: If these principles could change my life, imagine the impact they could have on others. That thought planted the seed for this book. My goal is simple—to share what I've learned so that you don't have to hit the wall before finding your path to both success and happiness.

How will this book help you?

In 2014, despite having over 20 years of work experience and holding senior leadership roles, I realized I still hadn't found the joyful balance between work and life. That insight was both humbling and eye-opening.

As a teacher at an MBA program, I observe many young students—just starting out in their careers—already struggling with the same dilemma. They graduate full of energy and ambition, yet within just a few years in the industry, many feel the weight of imbalance pulling them down. On the other end of the spectrum, I've also met seasoned professionals in their forties who experience a midlife crisis, questioning whether all their hard work is truly worthwhile.

This book is intended for working professionals aged 25 to 50 years. These 25 years are the most productive phase of one's career. These 25 years aren't just about building a career—they are about laying the foundation for lifelong success and happiness, in both work and life. If we get this balance right, the next 50 years of life can be lived with joy.

How is this self-help book different?

Self-help books in this space generally fall into four categories:

1. The Academic Lens – Written by professors who conduct extensive research and share valuable theories, but often lack deep, lived corporate experience.
2. The Entrepreneur's Perspective – Written by founders who've built businesses and achieved great success yet face challenges very different from those of professionals navigating corporate careers.
3. The New-Age Gurus – Focused on Eastern wisdom such as mindfulness, meditation, and spirituality. While deeply enriching, they sometimes miss the practical hacks needed to thrive in today's fast-paced corporate world.
4. The Corporate Survivor's Voice – Books written by professionals who have lived through the grind themselves, faced the pressures, survived, and emerged stronger—with lessons to share.

Each type of book has its own strengths. My book belongs to the fourth category. I have experienced these struggles first-hand, overcome them, and now share my journey of success and happiness—not from theory, but from practice.

Why might I be uniquely qualified to write this book?

I'm not a billionaire entrepreneur like Bill Gates (Microsoft) or Mukesh Ambani (Reliance). Nor am I a superstar CEO like Tim Cook (Apple) or Sundar Pichai (Google). Those leaders are true outliers who reached extraordinary heights.

I'm an ordinary, middle-class man who started his career as an Area Sales Manager in Madhya Pradesh—a small territory known more for its ravines (gullies) than its markets. From there, through steady effort and persistence, I climbed the corporate ladder to become a multi-geo global executive. Mine is quite literally a "Gully to Global" story.

I come from a middle-class family that believed in one timeless Indian principle: Saraswati (Learning) first, Lakshmi (Earning) next. Education was our foundation and the surest path to building a good life. I studied hard, graduated with distinction in Engineering and MBA, and earned a merit scholarship. Our dreams were simple, like most middle-class Indians; we believed in a good education, a steady corporate career, and raising a strong, values-driven family.

- Over three decades, my journey took me across diverse roles and geographies:
- Worked with Indian companies like Eicher Motors and HCL.
- Served in global IT multinationals like Digital, Compaq, and HP.
- Gained experience in the Middle East with Bahwan Auto in Oman.

- Lived in North and Central India (Delhi, Noida, Indore), South India (Bangalore, Chennai),
- Lived in East Asia (Singapore) and West Asia (Oman).
- Spent 15 years as an individual contributor, and another 15+ years as a manager and "manager of managers," leading directly teams across India, China, Japan, Korea, Australia, Southeast Asia, and beyond.

But what truly defines me are not just the roles or the titles—it is the hardships, setbacks, and persistence that shaped my journey. Nothing came easy. Every disappointment became a lesson. Every setback builds resilience. And every challenge tested and strengthened my tenacity. That is why I believe my story will resonate with most readers—especially those who, like me, left their hometowns in search of better opportunities, driven by the aspirations of an average middle-class professional.

As Shah Rukh Khan famously said, in a movie: "Don't underestimate the power of a common man." I am that common man. A corporate employee who has walked the long road to find not just success, but the joyful balance of work and life, achievement and happiness.

How will this book help you?

In today's world, where success is often glorified more than anything else, many professionals chase achievements while unknowingly sacrificing their health, happiness, and peace of mind. The relentless hustle, the pressure to outperform, and the constant grind have left countless young professionals and mid-career individuals feeling stressed, disillusioned, and stuck.

My book, Joyful Balance, is a guide to redefining success—showing how you can achieve your ambitions while also embracing joy, health, purpose, and personal growth. It draws from my own transformative journey—from corporate burnout to personal breakthrough—offering practical wisdom, powerful tools, and a Meta Mind six-step blueprint for creating a more balanced and fulfilling life.

I know this approach works. When I shifted my focus from chasing career milestones alone to pursuing my passions, they made me a happier person. Becoming a more balanced and happiness-focused person made me achieve more milestones that once seemed impossible, while keeping my family, finances, health, and inner joy intact.

- I completed three challenging Himalayan motorbike expeditions—Tawang, Darjeeling, and Ladakh—all after the age of 50, confronting my worst fears of cold, high altitude, and bad roads.
- I fulfilled a lifelong dream of teaching by designing and delivering a full-fledged university course on E-commerce for MBA students, dedicating 100+ hours a year to preparation, delivery, and evaluation.
- At HP Inc., I was honoured with the President's Club Award—the highest recognition for any sales executive.
- I received the Global Top 200 Marketer Award from White Page International, London.
- And I was humbled to be recognized with the Distinguished Alumni Award from my alma mater, BIM Trichy.

Each of these achievements is meaningful in its own right. But when viewed together—while maintaining balance in life—they represent something far more powerful. This state is called "Joyful Balance."

If you want more context and details on my career and life experiences, which shaped me, please refer to the section in the end - Nash Memoir – Joyful Balance in action.

What is Joyful Balance?

Joyful Balance is a state of true well-being—where work and life exist in harmony, and where success and happiness walk hand in hand. I experienced this transformation only after I chose to become a happiness-centric leader—someone who defined success on my own terms, embraced balance, and began to truly enjoy the journey.

The first balance is getting both success and happiness in one's professional life. For that reason, productivity alone is insufficient. To sustain success over such a long period, one must also find happiness at work.

The second balance lies beyond work. True joy comes from nurturing all aspects of life—health, finance, family, relationships, and community. In this book, I share how we can align purpose with passion and potential, create thoughtful plans, work meaningfully with others, and persist through challenges.

The best part is—you can achieve this too. Joyful Balance is not a distant dream; it is completely attainable. The key lies in knowing where to play (aligning with your purpose, passion, and potential) and how to win (through the proper planning, people, and persistence).

In this book, I will share with you the framework and the secrets to achieving both success and happiness—in work, life, and beyond. By applying these principles, you will be able to:

- Redefine success on your own terms by setting your top five life goals for the next decade.
- Build and follow a joyful blueprint for both work and life.
- Discover greater health, fulfilment, and clarity.
- Experience visible improvements in your relationships, career focus, and energy.

Before that, let's bust the myths and misconceptions of work-life balance, success, and happiness. Then let us examine what is stopping us from achieving the desired outcomes.

Chapter 3

THE MYTH OF "I'LL BE HAPPY LATER"

Busting the myths & roadblocks to joyful balance.

Before we can design a joyful, balanced life, we must first challenge the myths we've been told and remove the roadblocks we've built ourselves. Success and happiness are not distant cousins—they can and should walk together. Here are ten myths I had to bust on my own journey, and how you can too.

Myth 1: You CANNOT be both successful and happy.

We're conditioned to believe "no pain, no gain," as if joy and success can't coexist. Think of 1970s Hindi movies where the rich man in the bungalow was always corrupt, and success meant unhappiness. But in real life, I've met enough high-performing executives who are also genuinely happy. Success and happiness can thrive together when you design your life consciously.

Myth 2: Work-life balance is impossible.

Balance is often misunderstood as splitting hours equally between work, family, hobbies, and health. That's impossible. Balance works when *you* define it, not when society dictates it. I realised, balance is not about equal hours, but about alignment.

Myth 3: Success demands endless sacrifice.

We admire athletes such as Rafael Nadal for their discipline, assuming their lives are characterized by sacrifice. But Nadal once said he never sacrificed anything—he loved tennis. True success is joyful when we align it with our purpose and passion.

Myth 4: Money and material success define everything.

Chasing money alone is like driving fast without entering a destination in Google Maps. Without a holistic definition of success, you'll always feel lost, no matter how fast you move. Material success also brings some arrogance, rudeness, and brash confidence. I have experienced this; it harmed me. Thankfully, I completely changed later. And realised, wealth without health, family, and hobbies feels empty.

Myth 5: Comparing yourself to others helps you improve.

On a planet of 8 billion, no one has your exact fingerprint or path. Yet we waste energy comparing ourselves to peers— "My batchmate is ahead of me." True progress begins when you stop living by other people's opinions and start walking your own path. Our only competition is with our past self.

Myth 6: Career is everything.

Legendary investor Rakesh Jhunjhunwala admitted his "worst investment was his health." I've seen friends buy their dream

BMWs only to hire drivers because they weren't healthy enough to drive. Career is only one pillar—health and relationships matter as much.

Myth 7: Overwork proves your worth.

We think 70-hour weeks are the only way forward. But speed in the wrong direction is meaningless. Pausing to step back, reflect, and redirect often creates more impact than mindless effort. Working smarter beats just overworking.

Myth 8: Purpose and passion are only for dreamers.

Purpose isn't just for entrepreneurs or visionaries. A farmer feeding families or a teacher shaping minds also lives with purpose. Passion removes stress and fuels resilience. The purpose is for everyone.

Myth 9: Life can't be planned—it's too uncertain.

Yes, life throws curveballs. But when I had a plan—career, finances—I flourished. When I did not have a plan for health and hobbies,—I floundered. Even a simple 10-year vision provides direction. A flexible plan is better than drifting without one.

Myth 10: Relationships and hobbies can wait.

This may be the most dangerous myth. I've seen leaders reach the top only to find themselves alone, with no passions to share joy with. Never postpone joy—because without people and passions, success feels hollow. People and passions are not extras—they are the essence of life.

Final Thought

The myths hold us back; the truths set us free. Once you bust these myths and clear the roadblocks—comparison, overwork, blind chasing of money—you'll realize success and happiness don't compete. They complement each other. Balance is not only possible—it's the most powerful way to live.

Chapter 4

WHAT NO ONE TEACHES US ABOUT SUCCESS

Understanding Opportunities to succeed in the future

To plan, we must first understand the macro-environment and the megatrends that will shape it. While the future is uncertain, it also opens vast opportunities for career and business growth—because behind every challenge lies a hidden opportunity. In short, understanding *megatrends* is about understanding the Opportunities to win in the future.

Take climate change, for example. Global warming is one of the biggest challenges of our time. Yet, for companies working on clean energy—such as solar and wind—this challenge translates into enormous opportunities. One of my ex-managers used to say, "Behind every big problem is a big opportunity." He often cited how Indian IT services companies such as TCS, Infosys, and Wipro transformed the Y2K migration crisis into a billion-dollar industry.

Similarly, nations such as India and China have built a reputation for low-cost, frugal innovation, born of the constraints imposed by their status as developing economies with lower per capita incomes than those of the West. Necessity has always driven creativity and opportunity.

That's why one of the smartest approaches to thrive in a **VUCA (Volatile, Uncertain, Complex and Ambiguous)** world is to identify and ride the mega trends—to see opportunities where others only see difficulties. In my view, these are the most critical trends shaping our world through 2050.

1. Technology & AI:

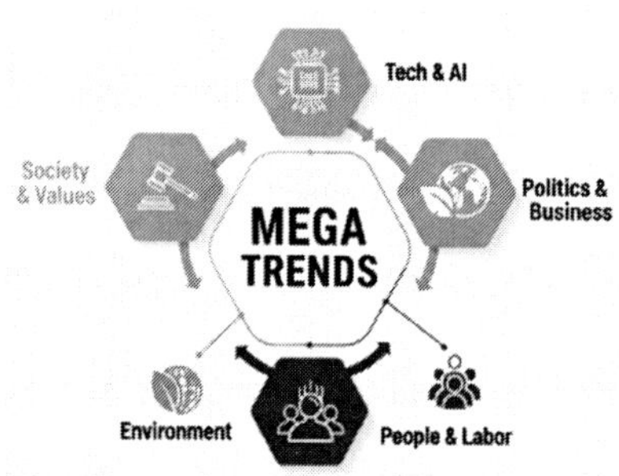

Tech and Artificial Intelligence have already transformed industries worldwide. While it brings challenges such as job displacement, ethical concerns, bias, and data privacy issues, it also unlocks tremendous opportunities in healthcare, finance, manufacturing, education, and beyond.

Take ChatGPT, for example—a conversational AI developed by OpenAI. It's based on the Generative Pre-trained Transformer (GPT) model, designed to understand and generate human-like text. It can answer questions, create content, translate languages, and assist with countless tasks. Essentially, the collective knowledge of humanity is now just a few keystrokes away.

But here's the real challenge: What questions will you ask? Knowledge is powerful only when you know how to use it. I'm reminded of a large English dictionary lying unused in a village school. The book was there, but no one had taught the children how to look up a word. Similarly, AI is only a tool—an incredibly powerful one—but it cannot replace human thinking.

In the age of AI, the most valuable skills will be those that complement technology rather than compete with it. Skills like:

- Critical thinking – to frame the correct problems and interpret answers.
- Emotional intelligence – to connect with people where machines cannot.
- Creativity and adaptability – to innovate and thrive in a changing world.
- Communication and collaboration – to lead teams, inspire action, and drive progress.

AI may excel at processing data and automating tasks, but humans remain essential for context, nuance, judgment, and ethics. That is where the future opportunities lie—for educators, healthcare professionals, counsellors, social workers, business strategists, consultants, managers, and leaders.

2. Politics and Business:

The world is already witnessing massive power shifts.

Just three decades ago, China and India were seen as poor, struggling economies—hardly considered among the global top 10. Today, their transformation has been nothing short of remarkable. Together, they have lifted over 900 million people out of poverty and integrated into the world's goods and services supply chain.

- China is now the world's second-largest economy.
- India stands at No. 5 and is projected to reach No. 3 by 2030.

India also holds a unique distinction—it is the world's largest democracy, where nearly a billion people participate in free and fair elections, peacefully changing governments every five years. This stands in stark contrast to much of the world, which remains dominated by monarchies, authoritarian regimes, one-party states, military dictatorships, or oligarchies.

For over 150 years (1850–2000), the global order was largely Western-centric, led by the US, Europe, Japan, and other industrialized nations. But the 21st century marks a clear shift of power toward Asia.

With nearly 45% of the world's population, Asia is set to play a dual role—as both a provider and a consumer of goods and services. This shift is already reshaping global trade, supply chains, and value creation.

For people in Asia, this isn't just a geopolitical change—it's a historic opportunity to harness talent, innovation, and economic growth on an unprecedented scale.

3. Environment & Climate Change:

Climate change is both a challenge and an opportunity. As industries grow and economies develop, pollution and resource exploitation are reshaping our environment in alarming ways. The average global temperature continues to rise due to global warming. Air quality is deteriorating annually, with AQI levels in many cities exceeding hazardous thresholds. Our planet's biodiversity is shrinking, with numerous species of flora and fauna threatened with extinction. Essential resources such as clean water, fresh air, oil, coal, sand, and rare-earth minerals are becoming increasingly scarce due to unsustainable extraction and overuse.

Yet, within this crisis lies a tremendous opportunity.

- Companies in the green energy sector—wind, solar, tidal, and green hydrogen—are poised for exponential growth.
- Sustainable farming methods that consume less water and energy will redefine agriculture.
- The recycling and circular economy will become massive industries.
- A major energy transformation is underway: shifting from fossil fuel dependency to renewable sources like wind, solar, geothermal, and tidal power.
- Even clean nuclear energy will play a supplementary role in reducing carbon reliance.

In short, the very challenges threatening our planet can open the door to innovation, entrepreneurship, and global collaboration—creating one of the biggest opportunities of our lifetime.

4. People, Education and Labour:

The world's population is projected to stabilize around 8 billion. However, the gap between the rich and poor will remain stark—and in many cases, widen. Even in developed countries, wealth is increasingly concentrated among a few, while vulnerable groups struggle to keep pace.

Nations like India and China—together home to 40% of humanity— are already global powerhouses in services and goods, respectively. Their continued rise will be driven by a massive middle class with growing purchasing power. Meanwhile, migration will persist, as people move to labour markets offering higher wages and better opportunities.

Education will carry a premium in specialized fields such as engineering, management, commerce, medicine, law, and biotechnology. Yet there will also be renewed respect for the fine arts, as well as for vocational skills such as plumbing, electrical work, and driving—practical abilities that will always remain in demand.

Healthcare, meanwhile, will become more expensive. The COVID-19 pandemic was a stark reminder of the fragility of the global health system. In the years ahead, elderly care and caregiving for the sick will pose both immense challenges and vast opportunities for professionals, entrepreneurs, and service providers alike.

The labour market will move more towards the gig economy, where gig workers are hired for specific tasks like short-term, flexible jobs and projects, or "gigs" rather than traditional full-time employment. Often facilitated by digital platforms connecting consumers with service providers, it allows businesses to access flexible labour on demand and workers to enjoy autonomy and variety but also presents challenges in income stability and worker protections.

5. Society and Values:

One of the greatest challenges we face today is the erosion of human values. Qualities such as kindness, tolerance, humility, patience, perseverance, and truth are increasingly being sacrificed at the altar of speed, materialism, and power.

Consider tolerance—the ability to engage in respectful dialogue with someone holding an opposing viewpoint. The art of "disagreeing agreeably" is fast disappearing. Instead, we see deep polarization everywhere: Right vs. Left, Nationalist vs. Liberal, BJP vs. Congress, Democrats vs. Republicans. Social media echo chambers amplify divisions, and TV debates often descend into noisy shouting matches rather than meaningful discussions.

Yet, within this challenge lies a profound opportunity. Around the world, countless organizations work selflessly toward peace and service to humanity. Whether it's a school or hospital run by the Ramakrishna Mission, Sathya Sai Trust, Sisters of Charity, or the Aga Khan Foundation, their service transcends religion, offering education and healthcare without discrimination. This is humanity at its very best.

Even corporations are waking up to this need. Many global technology companies, including HP, are actively working to bridge the digital divide and build sustainable, value-driven organizations. Increasingly, employees prefer to work for companies that align with their personal values, even if it means passing up higher salaries elsewhere.

The message is clear: while values are under pressure, they also present one of the greatest opportunities—to rebuild a society and workplaces anchored in purpose, compassion, and shared humanity.

For more details on mega trends, please refer:

https://www.rolandberger.com/en/Insights/Global-Topics/Trend-Compendium/

https://www.pwc.com/gx/en/issues/megatrends.html

Chapter 5

SUPER SKILLS REQUIRED TO SUCCEED IN THE FUTURE

Now that you understand the *megatrends* and the opportunities they create, the question is: how can you prepare for this future? The answer is simple: keep learning. Of course, you must master your work-related skills (like accounting if you're an accountant, or coding if you're an engineer). But beyond that lies something even more powerful: a set of super skills called *meta-skills.*

Meta-skills are higher-order, transferable skills that remain relevant throughout your lifetime. They are different from both Technical and Soft skills. Unlike technical skills, which may become outdated, meta-skills grow stronger with experience and adapt to any role, industry, or stage of life. And unlike, soft skills, where the focus is primarily on interpersonal and behavioural competencies, used to interact and perform tasks. Most importantly, they will be your most significant differentiator in the era of AI, where machines can take over routine tasks, but meta-skills remain uniquely human.

These meta-skills fall into three broad categories:

1. Self-skills
2. Social skills
3. Thinking skills

Let's dive deeper into each of these and explore how you can develop them.

1. Self-management skills

a. Initiative: Ability to take responsibility for your life, acting independently without being told.
b. Adapting: Ability to change to suit different conditions in an ever-changing work environment.
c. Integrity: Ability to be honest. Adherence to strong moral and ethical principles and values
d. Focus & Discipline: Ability to concentrate and manage your time and attention effectively.
e. Resilience: Ability to bounce back from mistakes and setbacks, viewing them as learning opportunities

2. Social intelligence skills

a. Feeling/ Empathy/ Emotional Intelligence: Ability to understand and manage emotions, both your own and others, and to respond appropriately.

b. Communicating: Ability to convey information effectively and understand others.
c. Collaborating: Ability to work effectively with others towards a common goal.
d. Leading: Ability to guide, motivate, and influence a group of people to achieve a shared goal.

3. Deep Thinking skills

a. Curiosity: Ability to learn and explore new ideas and information constantly.
b. Critical thinking: Ability to analyse info objectively, distinguish facts from opinions, and make judgments.
c. Creativity: Ability to think about problems in a new or different way. Using imagination to generate ideas
d. Problem-Solving: Ability to identify issues, develop strategies, and apply knowledge to find solutions.
e. Sense making: Ability to interpret disparate information and understand its meaning and significance.
f. Storytelling: Ability to connect with others through narratives.

We will have many opportunities in our lifetimes to learn and refine our meta-skills. I found the book, "What the Heck Do I Do with My Life?" authored by Ravi Venkatesan, an excellent book on this subject. You will find it a helpful read if you want to learn more about this subject.

PART 2

FOUNDATIONAL BELIEFS

"Your time is limited, so don't waste it living someone else's life. Don't let the noise of other's opinions drown out your own inner voice. Have the courage to follow your heart and intuition."

– Steve Jobs.

Chapter 6

IT ALL BEGINS AND ENDS IN HERE.

We began this journey by exploring the myths and misconceptions surrounding work-life balance, success, and happiness. Then, we looked at what really holds us back from achieving the life we desire. In my memoir at the end, you can read my own story—from gully to global—and how I grew not only as a corporate leader but also as a teacher, volunteer, motorcyclist, photographer, and writer.

But here's the truth: I wasn't always this way. Everything changed after 2015, following a period of burnout and depression. That phase prompted deep introspection. I began asking myself: What is truly working for me? What isn't? What beliefs and patterns of negative self-talk are sabotaging my growth?

With the support of my wife, Priya, and a few close friends, I gradually uncovered insights that I couldn't have seen on my own. They helped me step back, observe myself with objectivity, and re-examine my inner dialogue. This wasn't easy, but with their guidance, I realized that many of my deeply held beliefs were, in fact, limiting me rather than serving me.

So, I began the process of replacing those limiting beliefs with empowering ones. How did I know these new beliefs were correct? Because they made me feel lighter, calmer, happier, and deeply aligned within.

Over time, I distilled these lessons into 10 empowering foundational beliefs—born from my mistakes, refined through self-discovery, and tested in real life. They transformed me, and I believe they can transform anyone who chooses to adapt them.

1. Define your unique success path. Never compare.

Did you know there is no one else like you on this planet? Even identical twins have completely different fingerprints. You are truly one in eight billion—a superpower once you fully realize it.

For a long time, I made the mistake of comparing myself to others—college batchmates, cousins, colleagues. I thought I was benchmarking my career and life progress, but I ignored one crucial fact: every individual has a unique background, family situation, capabilities, and struggles. I would feel superior or inferior depending on who I compared myself to that day. These comparisons never brought happiness. Even when I was "ahead" of many peers, my heart felt restless—like trying to quench my thirst with seawater.

The reality of it hit me years later during a conversation with a colleague. His peer from long ago was now a global CEO, while he was "just a VP." When I asked if he ever felt bad, he laughed. He said he was content being a VP. Comparing himself to others only brought anxiety. The CEO, he explained, had a distinct trajectory, unique challenges, and was facing health and family struggles despite outward success. On a lighter note, he admitted he even felt a little pity for the CEO—but no envy.

He added a simple but profound thought: the only comparison that matters are with yourself—where you are today versus where you were yesterday. He was proud of his own journey: starting as a sales rep in a small town and growing to become VP of a major geography in a multinational company.

That hit me like a rock. I realized how much more productive and fulfilling it would be to focus my energy on improving myself, rather than measuring my life against others. If you've read my career story, Gully to Global, you'll see how far I've come. I may not be Sundar Pichai, who became Google's CEO, but I am Nash Narasimhan, proud of my own journey from Gully to Global.

This brings us to an important point: defining our own terms of success. Success is meaningless unless we define it for ourselves. For one person, it might mean leading a simple, honest life. For another, it could be a sea-facing villa and a convertible in the garage. For some, it's raising a family while staying close to their parents. For others, it might be good health and financial independence, or simply happiness and peace of mind. With a billion people on this planet, there are a billion different dreams. There is no universal definition of success—unless you define it for yourself.

By 2025, I had defined success on my own terms and created a plan that placed work-life balance and joy at its heart. Hence, I use the term "Joyful Balance." I visualized it as a hexagon with six edges, representing goals in Health, Happiness, Career, Care, Family, and Finance. I'll explore this in more detail in the chapter on planning.

I know I am unique. I know what makes me successful. Once you understand these two things, you unlock a tremendous personal power.

2. Happiness fuels success, not vice versa. Satisfaction beats success.

From a young age, we are gradually conditioned to believe that success comes before happiness. If you grew up in a middle-class family, like most of us, your parents probably told you: study hard to get into a good school, score well to get into a good college, excel in college to land a good job, perform well at work to earn promotions and raises, buy a nice car, and a good house, get married, have children… and the cycle continues.

Our parent's intentions are always good—they want their children to succeed and live well. But this mindset has a hidden cost: it teaches us to postpone joy indefinitely. We are made to believe that happiness and well-being are rewards for success, and that material achievement is the only path to fulfilment.

But pause for a moment—is this true? Why do we witness so many suicides in colleges, even at prestigious institutions like the IITs? Why are countless people unhappy in top jobs at the world's best companies? Why do so many marriages break down, children yearn for their parents' attention, and grandparents get abandoned? Why do people quit stable jobs to take year-long breaks, searching for happiness that success alone cannot deliver?

These questions reveal a fundamental truth: success without joy is incomplete. Happiness is not something to postpone; it is something to live and cultivate alongside success.

My story is similar. It was all OK till I got into a good job. But instead of enjoying the job for its intrinsic value and my contribution to company success, my focus shifted to what's next? What is the next move I need to make? How can I get promoted fast? I was on this hedonistic treadmill, where no amount of success at a young age was enough. It was always about what's next? Instead of enjoying and contributing to my job, it was about being seen as successful and contributing. Why? Because in my mind, I equated success with happiness, like many. I forgot how; success is an external measure, whereas satisfaction and happiness are internal feelings.

As a salesperson, my numbers and performance increasingly dictated my mood. If I had a good quarter, achieved my sales targets, and bonuses, I was happy. If I missed my numbers, due to unfavourable market conditions, even after working hard, I felt miserable, for no fault of mine. This showed in my interactions at home. A bad day at the office will be noted well by family members. I could not compartmentalize work pressure from home on many days. Has this happened to you?

This led to my eventual burnout in 2014. I held the title of APJ CMO. I had a BMW Car—a nice house. Good family and decent health. I had all outward success, but I felt hollow and unhappy inside. I was not happy. Thankfully, after one year of deep reflection and therapy, when I transformed myself into a happiness-centric leader, I started prioritizing my own job satisfaction and inner happiness over outward success markers like fancy titles, cars, houses, etc.

There are two books I would recommend you read. "The Happiness Advantage" by Shawn Achor. And "If you are so smart, why are you not happy?" by Raj Raghunathan. Both books show that the most successful people in the world have prioritized happiness and inner satisfaction over external success. In fact, Shawn Achor even suggests that happiness is an advantage and almost a prerequisite for sustainable success.

3. Reframe every challenge as an opportunity or adventure.

Every human being faces challenges every day, but how you respond shapes your happiness and success. Earlier, I used to get stressed over even minor things that didn't go as planned. Over time, I learned to approach life differently, guided by two key strategies.

First, treat life as an adventure. Imagine how boring life would be if it were predictable. The excitement comes from unpredictability, whether the outcome is good or bad. Face challenges head-on with a sense of curiosity and adventure. Don't worry excessively about the future—you can handle it well if you focus on the present. As a biker, I've learned this on long road trips: weather changes, bad roads, mechanical faults, or route errors can all go wrong. If I obsess over every possibility, I will never ride. But when I treat each ride as an adventure, every obstacle adds a little fun and action, making the journey memorable.

Second, see challenges as learning opportunities. Ask yourself: What is good about this challenge? What can I learn? What can I do right now?

For example, when I joined DEC in 1997, Compaq acquired the company within a year. Many feared job losses. I asked my manager how to handle it. He advised: "Focus on your current work, do it well, learn about the new company, explore new opportunities, and embrace the change. Things will take care of themselves." By following this advice, rather than worrying, I put in my best efforts, learned the new organization, and was eventually promoted.

A similar situation happened in 2007, during the financial crisis. HP acquired EDS, resulting in significant redundancies. My hardware role became redundant, and I had the chance to move into services, a completely new area for me. I hesitated, unsure if I could succeed. A friend gave me simple but powerful advice: "Nash, treat this service job as a learning opportunity—like joining a university course. Approach it with a learner's mindset, and you'll do well." I followed this guidance, and by 2008, India became HP's best-performing country for services globally.

All of this taught me that when you convert difficulties into opportunities to learn, challenges transform from obstacles into stepping stones for growth.

4. Think positive, dream big, and convert negative self-talk to positive.

In my 30+ years of work, I've noticed a clear pattern among all successful and happy people: they are optimists. They think positively and dream big. This doesn't mean they are unrealistic—they analyse their strengths, weaknesses, opportunities, and threats (SWOT), understand where they stand, and yet maintain a positive mindset and ambitious vision. In all my experience, I have yet to meet a truly successful pessimist.

Personally, I always look for opportunities amid difficulties. Failures, in my view, are simply stepping stones to success. For instance, I didn't pursue electronics engineering, my preferred branch, yet it didn't prevent me from building a career in the IT industry. I didn't make it into IIM-Ahmedabad despite clearing the tough CAT exam, yet I eventually became APJ CMO for a multi-billion-dollar business.

This comes from converting negative self-talk into positive thinking. When I missed my favourite branch, I reminded myself that even Steve Jobs wasn't an engineer, yet he built one of the world's biggest computer companies. When I didn't get into IIM-A, I thought about Dhirubhai Ambani, who built Reliance, India's largest company, without an MBA.

This approach—what I call "Swap Thinking"—turns setbacks into motivating self-talk and fuels growth. Observe all great leaders: they convert difficulties into opportunities. Being thrown out of a first-class compartment in South Africa, despite having a ticket, might crush someone else—but M.K. Gandhi turned it into a pivotal life lesson, fought for the oppressed, and eventually helped bring down the British Empire in his lifetime.

Remember, the best answer is extraordinary success, and that comes from positive self-talk, dreaming big, and taking bold action.

5. The best investment is in oneself.

The great investor Warren Buffett was once asked what his best investment was. He replied something along the lines of: "In myself—by reading books and learning from others."

I relate deeply to this. Coming from a middle-class family, my father was the sole financial provider and ensured that his three children were well-educated on a modest income. I was the youngest. By the time I graduated as an engineer, my father had retired. I received a campus placement offer, but I was also selected for an MBA program in another city, which would entail higher expenses due to tuition and hostel fees. Living on his pension post-60, my father hesitated to fund it.

That's when my mother stepped in. She didn't see this as an expense; she saw it as an investment in my future. She convinced my father to fund my MBA from his meagre savings. That tough decision transformed my life. The opportunities and earning potential I gained after my MBA were on a completely different level, and I am forever grateful to my parents for taking that leap of faith.

Another example: in 2019, almost 30 years after my MBA, I enrolled at ISB Hyderabad for a six-month course on Digital Transformation. It cost money, but it was an investment I made in myself. That course proved invaluable, when I led the digital transformation of 600+ HP World retail stores just before COVID-19 hit. Likewise, I did other programs to invest in myself. Some company sponsored like in IIM-Bangalore (Leadership) and INSEAD-Singapore (Channel management). Some on my own, with Adam Khoo in Singapore, Patterns of Excellence (POE) training based on Neuro Linguistic Programming (NLP). Another one with Adam Khoo on attaining financial independence through prudent wealth management. And with Avinash Ananda, to become an Internationally certified meta-mind international leadership and happiness coach. Investing in myself through these learnings, helped me immensely, to grow into a successful marketing, digital professional and people leader.

Education doesn't have to be formal university programs. In today's world, digital learning opportunities are immense. All it takes is curiosity and the willingness to learn. Keep learning, keep growing, and as I've emphasized earlier, continually enhance your *meta-skills*.

6. Work-life balance, pyramid or radar chart.

For nearly two decades, I believed that a career was the foundation of a good life. To an extent, that's true—but the problem arises when career becomes the only thing in your life. Career growth cannot come at the cost of your health, happiness, family, hobbies, or peace of mind.

There are two persistent myths:

- If I have a successful career, I will be happy.
- I can take care of my health, family, and relationships later in life.

I know this firsthand. I once pushed my career so hard that I experienced burnout and depression. Looking back, I had to ask myself: Was it worth it? Sadly, many young people today age visibly, before 30, and some even succumb to work-related stress before 40.

Our lives are worth far more than our careers. A career is just one part of the pyramid of life. When done well, it can approach the apex, but it can never form the base. Without good health, happiness, and balance, it's impossible to sustain a successful long-term career.

The key is clear: balance, not obsession, is the foundation of a fulfilling life.

Chapter 7

THE COST OF IGNORING BALANCE

To understand the concept of balance in life, consider the analogy of buying a smartphone. A perfect phone would ideally have six features: long battery life, large screen, compact design, great camera, blazing performance, and low price.

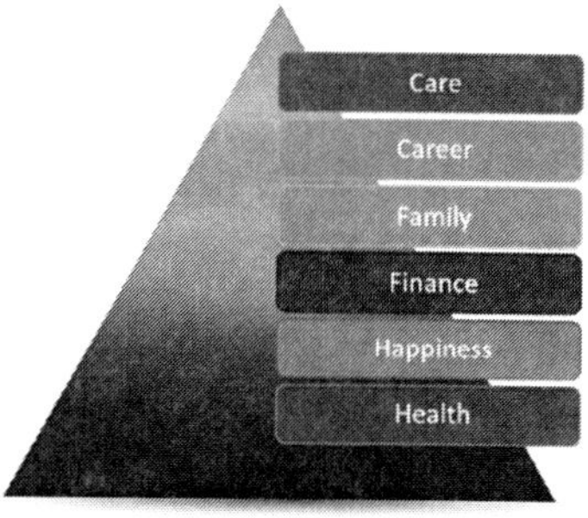

But here's the catch: you intuitively know that some features contradict each other. A big battery and a large screen make the phone less compact. A great camera and high performance usually come at a higher price. No phone can score 10/10 on all six features.

So how do you make the best decision? You assign a percentage or priority to each feature and decide what you can accept as a minimum. For example, your ideal battery life might be 2 days, but you can live with 1 day. Apply the same thinking to each feature.

Finally, you choose the optimal combination that maximizes overall value for your unique needs. This is the power of balance—making thoughtful trade-offs to achieve the best overall outcome, rather than obsessing over perfection in every single aspect. See the radar chart picture below.

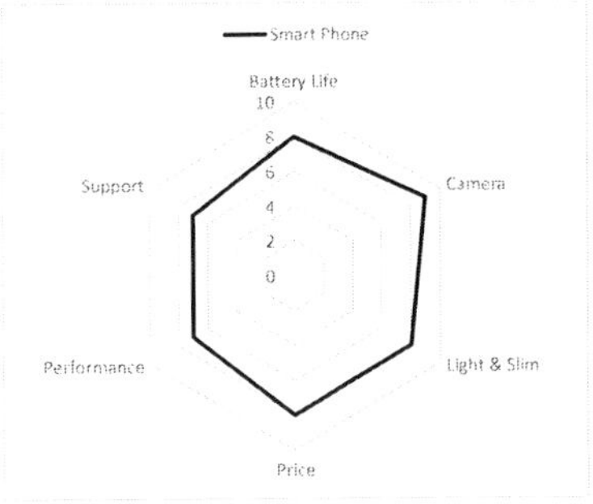

Likewise, in life, we need to have 360° goals, covering all six areas of life below.

1. Health (or Physical goals)
2. Happiness (Or Emotional goals)
3. Career (Or Professional goals)
4. Care (Or Spiritual or Service goals)
5. Family (or Social or relationship goals)
6. Finance (Or Material goals)

The framework for Joyful Balance could be Happiness, Health, Career, Care, Family, and Finance—or $H^2C^2F^2 = (HCF)^2$.

Imagine these six elements as the edges of a hexagon. Just like in life, you cannot score 10/10 on all edges simultaneously. You define your own success criteria, guided by your heart and unique circumstances.

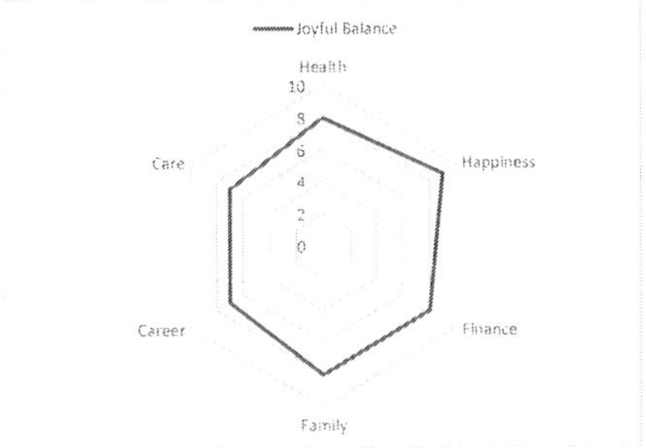

I only began thinking this way in my mid-forties—though I could have started at 25. No one coached me at the time, but now I can share this insight with you. I decided to aim for a minimum of 60% of my ideal in each area, while allowing myself to achieve 80% or 100% in some areas depending on priorities.

For example, in my mid-forties, while serving as APJ CMO, I was about 90% of my career ideal, but only 30% in health, 50% in finance, 40% in family and relationships, and 10% in community service. I made a conscious decision to step back slightly from my career and invest more energy in other areas, gradually bringing greater balance to my life. Refer later section on "My Actionable worksheet No. 3"

Started working on my health, family, hobbies, finance, community, and this in turn helped me do well in my career too. I can say that, after a few years, I was scoring more than 70% on the six parameters that were vital to me. In Business terms, this is also called the balanced scorecard. Suppose revenue, profit, and market share are key to business success. There is no point in focusing only on revenue at the expense of profits, or on profits at the expense of market share; we need all three, and we track our progress using the balanced scorecard. Balance is life's balance scorecard. Never let your career dictate your life satisfaction index.

7. Collecting the Gold coins (not just silver coins) in life

"Not all things worth counting are countable, and not all things that count are worth counting," said Albert Einstein.

I had the privilege of working with an exceptional manager at HP, an American, Global Marketing VP, named Michelle Weiss. She led a team of services marketing people, across three regions of AMS, EMEA and APJ. I led her APJ team. She once told us, "Focus on collecting gold coins in life, not just silver coins." Naturally, we asked her what she meant.

She explained: silver coins are the easily measurable things—your title, salary, team size, marketing budget, sales quota, house, or car. These can be compared, quantified, and often become the focus of our ambitions.

Gold coins, on the other hand, are more complex—or even impossible—to measure: love, respect, compassion, motivation, morale, trust, and integrity. Michelle taught us to focus on the gold coins, the truly valuable things that shape people and teams, rather than just numbers on a spreadsheet.

Her life was a testament to this philosophy. As WW VP of Marketing for HP's services business, she didn't have the biggest team or the most significant budgets. Yet her team consistently led in creativity, energy, team spirit, and morale—qualities that are harder to measure but far more impactful.

Her influence was profound: none of us wanted to leave her team, even when bigger roles came our way. She demonstrated through her actions that focusing on the gold coins leaves a legacy that numbers alone cannot create. Likewise in the journey of life, many tend to focus on collecting the silver coins like big house, fancy car, huge bank balance, great titles etc. We miss collecting the real gold coins like happiness, love of family, company of friends, the joy of good health, a clear conscience, respect of colleagues, standing up for your values etc. A mentees or student's heartfelt thank you note is GOLD, but getting a raise is just SILVER. Once I decided to become a happiness-centric leader, my focus shifted to collecting more gold coins and fewer silver coins.

8. Hard work and action speak louder than words.

In a world full of glib talkers, the people who truly stand out are doers.

Take Kapil Dev, for example. When he started his career, he could barely speak English. Unlike many of his teammates from large cities such as Delhi or Mumbai, Kapil hailed from Haryana, where cricket was hardly a mainstream sport. If you've seen the film *1983*, several humorous scenes highlight his struggles with English and public speaking. But none of that mattered when he led India to victory in the 1983 ODI Cricket World Cup. The nation celebrated, and decades later, the prestigious Wisden named him the Indian Cricketer of the Century, ahead of stalwarts such as Gavaskar and Tendulkar. Even Gavaskar has often said that Kapil's leadership during the 1983 triumph was one of the finest moments of his career.

Similarly, during my APJ role at HP, I recall a meeting where the Australian team, had missed their quarterly sales target, presented a detailed slide deck explaining why they fell short. Everyone listened patiently. Then, in the nest meeting, came the Japanese team. Their English was limited, but their slide said it all: they had achieved 105% of their target and grown 10% in a market that grew only 4%. The result? Applause from everyone—including Australians, Chinese, and Indians. Despite poor English communication skills of the Japanese team, the impact of their actions was crystal clear to everyone.

These examples highlight a simple truth: actions speak louder than words. Successful and happy people are those who do, not just talk. That's why figures like Gandhi, Sathya Sai Baba, Mother Teresa, Aga Khan, JRD Tata, and Dhirubhai Ambani are remembered long after their passing—their actions, ideas, and institutions endure.

In both life and business, performance beats pedigree, and action always speaks louder than words. That is the most accurate measure of a person.

9. Acceptance, and not getting what you want, is also good luck.

Life doesn't always follow our plans—it often follows a divine plan. Sometimes, not getting what you want is a stroke of luck in disguise.

Take Sachin Tendulkar, for example. He initially wanted to be a fast bowler but got rejected. That very rejection led him to focus on batting, eventually making him the greatest batsman of all time. Or consider the tech industry: in 1998, Yahoo rejected Google for just $1 million. Today, Yahoo is barely relevant, while Google is a multi-trillion-dollar company.

In my own life, I experienced similar "setbacks" that turned out to be blessings in disguise. In 1990, during my MBA campus placement, I lost the final interview at a prestigious Indian IT firm. My first job posting was in the Hindi heartland of Madhya Pradesh, even though I didn't know a word of Hindi. At the time, I wanted one thing and got another—and I struggled to accept it.

Looking back, those apparent setbacks were exactly what prepared me for future success. The rejection from the IT firm pushed me into the auto industry, where I learned firsthand how IT products and services were used by customers. The experience in Madhya Pradesh enabled me to learn Hindi and successfully manage sales in a challenging market. These experiences directly led to my appointment as Country PC Category Manager for Compaq India, the world's No. 1 PC company at the time—before I even turned 30.

Without those early setbacks, I wouldn't have gained the experiences needed to succeed later. With time and perspective, I've learned to see results—especially unexpected ones—as divine blessings or strokes of good luck.

10. Good Karma, reap as you sow, the giver's mindset.

This is perhaps one of the most important beliefs that has shaped me as a person, and I owe it to my parents, who were incredible role models.

We all make mistakes, and sometimes we may hurt someone unknowingly—that is forgivable. We can apologize, make amends, and move on. But wilfully hurting others or engaging in immoral or unethical activities—even if they promise short-term gains—carries consequences that will catch up with us over time. I've seen influential senior executives, tyrannical in their behaviours, lose their positions, prestige, and influence rapidly. Conversely, I've seen junior employees who consistently do good work rise steadily to become MDs or VPs. You reap what you sow. If you consistently act with kindness toward others—customers, partners, relatives, friends—it comes back to you in countless ways. Harm others, and harm will eventually return. Do good, be good. Karma always catches up.

This brings me to the concept of the Giver's Mindset. In life, we constantly give and take. Broadly, people fall into three categories:

1. Takers – Those who see life as a zero-sum game: for them to win, someone else must lose.
2. Matchers – Those who treat life like a transaction: they give something only to get something in return.
3. Givers – Those who are special. They give far more than they take and often expect nothing in return. This selfless giving makes givers rare in a world dominated by self-interest.

Adam Grant, professor of management and psychology at Wharton, defines the values of these types: takers value wealth, power, pleasure, and winning; givers value compassion, helpfulness, responsibility, and social justice. In both organizational and life contexts, thoughtful givers tend to outperform matchers and takers in the long run.

I've experienced this personally. People with a giver's mindset are often the most successful, balanced, and happy. Need proof? Look at India's biggest philanthropists—Ratan Tata, Shiv Nadar, and Azim Premji. They built large companies such as the Tata Group, HCL, and Wipro, funded world-class universities, and led lives of purpose and contentment. But you don't need to look that far. Observe your own family, friends, or colleagues: those who are truly successful and happy are often net givers, people whose generosity and kindness define them.

Practice time. Go to the later section, "Applying Joyful Balance."

Refer to Actionable Worksheet 1 – Empowering Beliefs.

Examine and remove any negative self-beliefs that are harming you. And adapt empowering beliefs in your work and life. You can think along the lines of "Stop, Start, and Continue". What can I stop doing that is harming my journey to Joyful Balance? What must I start doing, and what can I continue doing, to achieve a joyfully balanced life of Happiness and Success in Work and Life?

PART 3

THE SIX FORCES THAT SHAPE A JOYFUL LIFE

The Meta Mind Six-Step framework for joyful balance

Let us see what we have learnt so far. First, we covered the myths and misconceptions of work-life balance, success, and happiness. We then examined what is preventing us from achieving the desired outcomes. Next, we examined foundational beliefs and ideas essential to a successful and fulfilling career and life. Now, let us understand the Meta Mind Six-Step framework, which will help you achieve joyful balance.

While all the examples are my own, I have leveraged this framework from the productivity and positivity workshop conducted by my Guru Avinash Ananda of Meta Mind International. Thank you, Avinash.

The Meta Mind Six Steps are outlined in the graphic below:

I shall explain each step above first in the context of work and then in life.

Chapter 8

PURPOSE: REDEFINE OR REDISCOVER YOUR "WHY".

"He Who Has a Why to Live Can Bear Almost Any How," Friedrich Nietzsche, German philosopher.

On one of my motorcycle trips through South India, I once saw two small children, a sister (~8 years) and her brother (~5 years), playing in a village. The small girl was carrying the even younger boy on her back, who would have been quite a load on her back and shoulders. I was worried it would hurt the girl and asked her, "Carrying him on your back, does it not hurt you?" For that, the girl replied, "No. It's a joy. He is my younger brother; I love him very much. And he is very happy when I carry him on my back. And that joy in him makes me forget how heavy he is," I reflected on this episode many times in my career. Whenever we go through difficult times, ask this question. Why are we doing this? If you have a good purpose, no amount of hard work will hurt you.

Was it easy for Gandhi and Mandela to be in jail for several years? Was it easy for Mother Teresa to work with the diseased and homeless people? Was it easy for Sathya Sai Baba to work with poor, malnourished, illiterate, and sick people? Was it easy for Jamshedji Tata to build the finest steel plants in the early 1900s when the world refused India the technology? What was common in all this? A strong purpose. Gandhi wanted independence for his country from British colonial atrocities. Mandela wanted social justice for blacks, who were treated badly by whites. Mother Teresa wanted to serve the poor. Sathya Sai Baba sought to eliminate malnutrition, illiteracy, and disease among his people and built state-of-the-art nutrition programs, schools, colleges, and hospitals to serve the needy. Jamshedji Tata recognized that steel was the backbone of industrial development and sought to promote his country's prosperity through local steel production. All of them had a very strong purpose. That helped them navigate life's difficulties. How about we leverage this power of purpose for our own lives and careers? The bigger the purpose and the higher the action, the better the results in your life. Let me illustrate with a few examples from my career and life.

i) Power of purpose for work.

Having the right perspective on your role can elevate your sense of purpose at work. Consider the famous Vidhana Soudha in Bangalore, which serves as the seat of the Karnataka State Legislature. Built from 1951 to 1956, it symbolizes democracy.

During construction, three masons were asked what they were doing. The first said, "I am laying bricks," the second, "I am building a wall," and the third, "I am contributing to one of the finest monuments of democracy." Although all three perform the same task, only the third worker has a meaningful perspective, elevating his work to a higher purpose. This outlook naturally makes him happier and more dedicated, leading to better performance.

I once had an operations executive on my team who handled all customer escalations related to delays and incorrect shipments. With thousands of orders processed daily, even a 0.5% dissatisfaction rate results in hundreds of upset customers. While we generally manage escalations well, festive seasons like Diwali bring increased order and delivery loads nationwide, often leading to more complaints and social media abuse, which can embarrass us and require urgent resolution. This individual remained exceptionally calm and patiently addressed every issue, never displaying frustration, even when faced with harsh language. Curious, I asked him how he maintained such composure. He replied, "Nash, the customer has spent their hard-earned money on a HP PC or Printer. They expect timely delivery. If we don't deliver on time, who else can solve that problem but me?" He viewed himself not just as an operations worker fulfilling orders but as a customer advocate within the company. His perspective transformed his role into a higher purpose, demonstrating the power of ownership and empathy.

Another tip is to join effective teams within companies with ambitious goals. I was fortunate to be part of several teams whose managers set ambitious goals. I will give just two examples to illustrate this point. In 1999, Compaq India (now HP India) set an audacious goal to launch India's first online store for PC within one year. Imagine the odds. In 2000, in India, a Desktop PC cost Rs. 50K, which was roughly equivalent to a year's salary for the average Indian. Laptops were above Rs. 2.0 Lakhs. PC penetration was less than 1% for a billion-plus population. Smartphones had not been invented yet. The cost of a good cell phone was above Rs. 50K. Cell phone calls cost Rs. 17 per minute. The average internet connection speed with a dial-up modem was 56 kbps.

The only e-commerce companies in India were online media companies like Rediff, Times, and SIFY, selling cakes and flowers which cost under Rs. 1,000 ($20 then). How crazy (or cutting-edge) must you be to decide to launch an online store ONLY for PCs in India? Compaq was crazy! And how crazy must a person be to give up a prized category job and jump into an unknown online business GTM, which was just a project plan on paper? I was crazy. All crazy forces conspired to launch India's first online store for PCs - the Compaq Cooldukaan (cool shop).

In one year, we sold over 600 PCs online at an average selling price of Rs. 1.00 Lakh, yielding almost 6 Crores in online revenue, making us the largest online store in India across any category. First time, any company in India handled sales of such high value via e-commerce purely on the trust of the brand name Compaq. I started crying with joy when the first customer, a lady, wrote in an email that she loves the orange Color Compaq Presario PC, with JBL speakers hanging on the side, and it reminded her of her Dog, which had big ears like our PC speakers.

Why am I telling this story? We just had a project plan on paper. Still, we had a BIG Audacious purpose to create India's first online store for PC's – and we executed it in a record time from building the website, integrating with our factory operations, setting up the call center, last mile delivery, logistics, online payment collection, to order tracking and digital marketing. Remember, this is more than 25 years ago, in 1999, and it was considered a very pioneering work in the Indian market. That is the power of purpose in action.

Another example is how we grew our PC business 10x over just 8 years. A great example of a team with a strong purpose and audacious goals, executing to perfection.

In summary, if you must GROW your career, have the right perspective for your job, have a BIG purpose and be part of teams which set Audacious goals.

ii) Power of purpose for life.

We saw how a strong purpose helps you grow in your career. Likewise, a strong sense of purpose elevates one's life to a different level. Before that we must learn to compartmentalize. On a train, we have several compartments, including passenger compartments, pantries, kitchens, and goods compartments. What will happen if we begin loading goods such as coal and steel into the passenger compartment? Or should all passengers sleep in the pantry? We never let that happen; we compartmentalize and learn to keep different things in different compartments. Similarly, never let a career dictate your outlook on life. These are two distinct compartments in life. There is LIFE beyond work.

Unless we develop our health, wealth, relationships with family and friends, joyful hobbies, and a sense of caring for others, our life is unidimensional, lacking balance, and hence incomplete.

You might be wondering: Where do I find the time to do all this? Doesn't it affect my work performance? Let me answer with my own experience.

For over two decades, until 2014, work completely defined my life. My days began at 8:30 a.m. and often ended only by 9:30 p.m. I easily spent more than 10 hours in the office each day, excluding travel time. Saturdays were no different—I'd put in another 4–6 hours. On average, I worked approximately 60 hours per week.

In fact, if I ever reached home by 6:30 p.m., my wife would jokingly ask, "Is today a half-day?" 😊 That's how abnormal had become "normal" for me.

While the expectation was a 40-hour work week, I was regularly putting in 20 hours more—convinced that without me, the organization couldn't run. The truth? Every employee, no matter how talented, is replaceable. Even if a CEO leaves, a successor is named within weeks. If something were to happen to me, my company would move on instantly. But for my family and loved ones, my absence would be an irreplaceable loss.

Sadly, this realization did not sink in at the time. I neglected hobbies, friends, and even family time. My health suffered—erratic meals, lack of sleep, no exercise, and rising stress. Yes, I was achieving professional milestones: winning sales awards, being recognized as top talent, and becoming APJ CMO before turning 40. But at what cost?

I couldn't separate my work and personal life. In my mind, work success equalled life success, and work failure meant life failure. A bad sales quarter didn't just stay in the office—it spilled over into my home, affecting my mood, my behaviour, and my relationships. The toll was heavy—not just on me, but on my family too.

When I repurposed my life from being work-centric to life-balanced, I began setting very different goals.

I developed a plan for my health—losing excess weight, eating more healthfully, walking 40 minutes a day, and starting each morning with meditation. I consciously invested in relationships—spending more time with family and reconnecting with friends.

I revived long-lost passions, like weekend motorcycle rides that always gave me joy. I also found meaning in giving back—through community service with the Sathya Sai Seva Organization, mentoring young professionals in the workplace, and teaching E-commerce as a university faculty member.

Interestingly, I still worked the standard 40 hours a week, but something had shifted—my quality of work skyrocketed. Tasks that previously required 60 hours now fit comfortably within 40 hours, with improved outcomes. My productivity increased, my stress reduced, and I found time for family, health, hobbies, and service.

The outcome? I was calmer, healthier, more creative, and more fulfilled. I slept better, felt more energized, and reported far higher life satisfaction than in my earlier years, when work was my sole obsession.

How did all this happen? Because I chose to repurpose my life—not for one-dimensional success at work, but for a joyful balance across all areas of life.

Another powerful way to repurpose your life is by cultivating an abundance mindset.

This is related to—but slightly different from—the giver's mindset I discussed in the foundational beliefs section. An abundance mindset is the belief that there are enough resources, opportunities, and successes in the world for everyone to thrive. Instead of focusing on scarcity or competition, it encourages optimism, generosity, and a focus on what is possible.

With this mindset, you develop a sense of security, gratitude, and confidence in limitless possibilities. It also serves as the foundation for achieving a balanced joy—because to succeed in multiple areas of life (work, health, family, hobbies, community), you must first believe that it is possible. You must trust that there are enough time, energy, and support within yourself and around you to make it happen.

That belief—that there is always "enough"—is what the abundance mindset is all about. And the good news is, it can be nurtured by consciously practicing a few simple habits.

1. Be thankful for all the things you have in life. (Like Eyesight, Working limbs etc)
2. Be mindful. Enjoy small pleasures (Like a nice walk or a good cup of tea)
3. Live life in the now. Yesterday is history. Tomorrow is a mystery. (Appreciate today's weather)
4. Swap your negative self-talk for positive ones. (Swap "I am always late" to "I always arrive on time")
5. Look for opportunities, rather than problems. ("This place is dirty" to "How can I make it cleaner?")
6. Celebrate other achievements and make others successful. (Compliment others good work publicly)
7. Give your knowledge and resources to others who need them. (Teach, mentor, coach younger colleagues)

If you change your life purpose to leading a more balanced life with an abundance mindset, you will change dramatically for the better. I am a living proof.

Practice time. Go to the later section, Applying Joyful Balance. Refer to Actionable Worksheet 2: Meta Mind Six-Step Framework.

For this area of Purpose, think and jot down what you can apply in your work and life areas.

Chapter 9

PASSION: WHAT ENERGIZES AND FULFILS YOU.

"Success comes to those who dedicate everything to their passion in life. To be successful, it is also very important to be humble and never let fame or money travel to your head."

– A. R. Rahman,

Oscar and Grammy winning music composer.

i) Power of passion for work.

Passion is a powerful emotion that drives action. It is the energy that fuels you and the source of deep fulfilment. Think of countless actors who arrived in Mumbai, the hub of Hindi cinema, with almost nothing—yet went on to achieve greatness despite overwhelming odds. What propelled them forward? Passion.

Consider athletes who wake up at 4:00 a.m. every day to train relentlessly—whether it's Sachin Tendulkar perfecting his batting or Neeraj Chopra rising from humble beginnings to become an Olympic gold medallist. Their stories prove a simple truth: passion, when combined with hard work and grit, can overcome any obstacle. Passion is not merely a feeling—it is the force that drives perseverance, continuous learning, and eventual success.

Now, let's bring this into the corporate world. My advice to anyone starting their career is this: eventually, follow your passion. I always wanted to work in the computer industry, but circumstances led me to the automotive sector for the first five years of my career. When I finally got my break in IT as a product manager, I was nervous—I was entering an industry I barely knew. Yet my passion for the role pushed me through the challenges and helped me excel.

Throughout my career—whether in category management, sales, marketing, services, channels, or e-commerce—I never took on a role I wasn't passionate about. That passion was evident to everyone around me. Why does this matter? Because passion makes work enjoyable, gives you the energy to overcome challenges, and sustains you when the odds are stacked against you. Passion, combined with patience, makes you unstoppable. Life is too short to live someone else's dream—so choose what excites you, even if the pay is modest at first.

A passionate person also adapts the mindset of "learn first, earn later." In the early stages of a career, the focus should be on gaining knowledge and experience rather than chasing rewards. I took on some of the toughest assignments—sales manager in remote areas, product manager for a challenger brand, launching an online store and call center, driving regional pricing strategy, and even leading integration during a mega-merger. These roles didn't always come with high pay, but they gave me invaluable lessons in leadership, resilience, and problem-solving. The financial rewards came much later—but the foundation of my success was laid by passion-fuelled learning.

ii) Power of passion for life.

In life, it's important to discover what excites you, energizes you, and elevates you. One of the best ways to reconnect with your passion is through hobbies.

During my burnout and depression days, a friend once asked me, "What activities brought you joy when you were younger?" I paused, thought deeply, and replied: "Going on long motorcycle trips, capturing great photographs, and singing karaoke." He then asked a simple but powerful question: "So why did you stop?"

At that time, in my mid-forties, I blamed it on work and family responsibilities as the sole breadwinner. But he laughed and gave me examples: Prime Minister Vajpayee wrote poetry, MS Dhoni pursued his love for motorbikes, N. Chandrasekaran (Tata Group Chairman) is an avid runner, and Amitabh Bachchan writes blogs even amidst his busy schedules. If leaders, cricketers, business icons, and actors with packed calendars can make time for their passions, why can't I?

That was a turning point. I realized that hobbies aren't a luxury—they are fuel for joy, balance, and creativity. If we don't make time for them, we lose a part of ourselves. No matter how busy life gets, it's essential to carve out time for the things that truly light us up.

Every person must have three hobbies – one to develop their curiosity, another for service-oriented activities, and the third for health. All these must be accompanied by a spirit of acceptance of the individual's uniqueness.

I coined the acronym **CASH** – Curiosity, Acceptance, Service and Health.

You need CASH to be happy in life. Let us examine the four now in detail.

1. Curiosity:

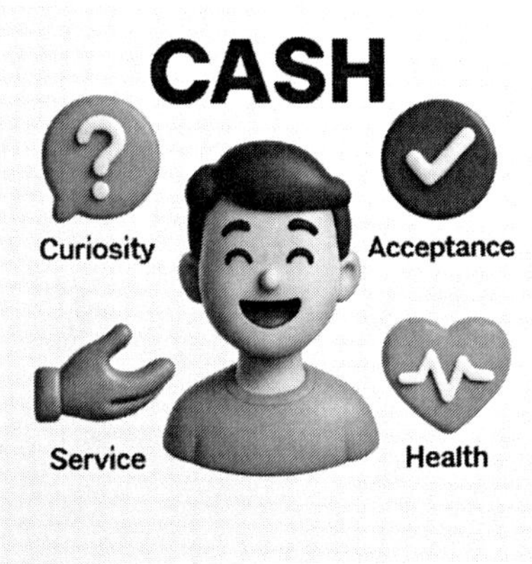

One powerful way to deepen your passion for life is by cultivating curiosity. Some of the greatest discoveries and inventions in history were born from nothing more than a curious mind. Albert Einstein once said, "Curiosity is more important than knowledge."

Why would a Nobel Prize–winning scientist, who had more knowledge of physics than almost anyone else, say that? Because curiosity was the fuel behind his breakthroughs. His theory of relativity, which explained concepts like time dilation, was first imagined through simple thought experiments—not complex equations. Decades later, scientists demonstrated that those thought experiments were correct. His curiosity not only advanced science but also influenced modern innovations like nuclear power and GPS, which we use daily on our smartphones.

The good news? You don't need Einstein's level of intelligence to develop curiosity. All you need is the willingness to ask questions and the hunger to learn. Wonder how birds fly, how fish swim, how cars work, or how Google Maps guides you? The answers are literally at your fingertips—the entire knowledge of humankind is available on your smartphone. All it takes is curiosity to unlock it.

That's why being a lifelong learner is so vital. As the saying goes: "Live like today is your last day and learn like you are going to live forever." Curiosity keeps life exciting, growth continuous, and passion alive—until the very last day we are on this planet.

There are countless ways to nurture and expand your curiosity. You could learn to sing, pick up a new musical instrument, read both fiction and non-fiction, take classes in photography or cooking, or even dive into history, civics, arts, science, or your own religion that you may not have had time to explore when you were younger. Each of these pursuits can spark wonder and sustain your curiosity.

For me, photography has been that spark. Ever since I bought my first SLR camera in the early nineties, the subject has fascinated me. I've grown tremendously as a photographer simply by taking more pictures, refining my skills, and continuously learning. Photography, much like cooking, is an art everyone can appreciate—even those who may not practice it themselves. The feedback I received from friends and relatives over the years has helped me sharpen my eye and improve my craft. Most importantly, it keeps me curious about the world around me.

In addition to photography, I write three blogs—on leadership, Indian culture, and motorbiking. Together, photography and writing have strengthened what I call "meta skills": Curiosity, Creativity, Critical Thinking, and Sense-Making. These are not just hobbies; they are powerful tools that shape how I learn, grow, and view life.

2. Acceptance:

Acceptance of your uniqueness is one of the best ways to deepen your passion for life. Too often, we admire qualities in others while overlooking the gifts we already possess. Perhaps the grass looks greener on the other side. Someone with straight hair longs for curls, while those with curls dream of straight hair. People in cold countries wish for more sunshine, while those in sunny regions wish for snow. The wealthy sometimes crave the simplicity of a modest life, while those with modest means dream of wealth.

It's human nature to focus on what we lack, but we often forget that what we already have may be someone else's ideal. True joy comes from embracing who we are, rather than wishing to be someone else.

When you accept your uniqueness with grace, you unlock the ability to nurture it further. If you have a natural passion for singing, join a karaoke club and refine your talent. If you enjoy painting, dancing, teaching, or cooking—lean into it, practice it, and celebrate it.

What you love to do naturally is not an accident—it is part of your gift. The key is to recognize it, accept it fully, and keep improving. That's where passion truly flourishes.

3. Service:

Engaging in activities that require both your hands, and your head is a powerful way to cultivate a service-oriented mindset. Service doesn't always require big gestures—it can be as simple as teaching a child in your neighbourhood basic math or science, volunteering on weekends to serve home-cooked meals to the needy or even helping your local police by managing traffic for a couple of hours.

You can also collect used clothing and essential items for donation, plant trees to contribute to afforestation, or offer your professional skills—whether as a lawyer, doctor, accountant, or teacher—once a month, free of charge, to those who cannot afford them. Returning to your alma mater to give guest lectures is another meaningful way to give back.

Personally, I find immense joy in two service activities. I volunteer with the Sathya Sai Seva Organization, where I participate in Narayana Seva, serving home-cooked meals to the elderly and underprivileged. I also teach a complete e-commerce course at a business school, investing more than 100 hours in preparing lectures, delivering classes, and grading assignments. The small honorary compensation I receive goes directly to an educational charity close to my heart.

These activities not only bring me fulfilment but also strengthen my passion for life. More importantly, they sharpen the meta-skills of empathy and collaboration, qualities that enrich every aspect of living.

4. Health:

Invest in activities that strengthen both your body and mind. A healthy mind resides in a healthy body. Health is precious, and once lost, it is difficult to regain. Ask anyone living with high blood pressure, diabetes, heart problems, depression, kidney issues, or joint pain—they would gladly trade anything to go back and prevent it. Most of these conditions are preventable through a healthy diet, regular physical activity, and healthy habits from an early age.

If you've neglected your health, it's never too late to start. Find a hobby that enhances your physical and mental well-being. Meditation, yoga, or chanting can sharpen your mind and bring clarity. Walking, jogging, running, or going to the gym builds physical strength. Playing sports such as tennis, basketball, cricket, squash, pickleball, football, cycling, or motorcycling enhances both physical fitness and social engagement.

For example, I practice yoga, meditation, and chanting for 30 minutes every morning, walk 40 minutes four times a week, and go on a motorcycle ride every fortnight. These routines not only maintain my health but also enhance my energy, focus, and social collaboration skills. Health is the foundation that empowers everything else in life.

I would like to give an example of a mentee, Venkat* here. He had over 20 years of work experience. He was a reasonably successful manager of a large team. However, there was a sense of emptiness in him. He was looking for a deeper meaning in life. I spent a few sessions with him. I discovered he actually achieved most of the goals he set for himself at work. I advised him in later sessions to look for a few activities which will make him give back his knowledge to society. And also cultivate a hobby which will keep him physically fit. I am glad, he started running with his community and participated in a few 10km runs. He also helps people, especially elders, do their financial planning using his deep knowledge of the subject. He is much happier now with these hobbies, which give him a sense of purpose beyond his work. * Names changed to protect the mentees privacy.

Think about what the CASH activities you can do to improve your passion towards life?

Practice time. Go to the later section, Applying Joyful Balance. Refer Actionable Worksheet 2 – Meta Mind Six Step framework.

For this area of Passion, think and jot down what you can apply in your work and life areas.

Chapter 10

POTENTIAL -DISCOVER &MAXIMIZE YOUR UNIQUE STRENGTHS

"If we did all the things we are capable of doing, we would literally astound ourselves"

– Thomas Edison.

Potential is the ability to transform our unique talents into achievements that shape our future. Yet, unrealized potential is one of the most common phenomena in the world. Talent is abundant, but what truly matters is how we harness it—as it defines the course of our lives.

Take Thomas Alva Edison, widely regarded as one of America's most prolific inventors. He created groundbreaking devices in areas such as electric power, mass communication, sound recording, motion pictures, and early versions of the electric light bulb—innovations that profoundly shaped the modern industrial world.

What many people don't know is that Edison's childhood was far from easy. There's a famous story that, as a young boy, he once came home from school with a note for his mother. "Mom," he said, "my teacher gave me this paper and said only you should read it. What does it say?"

With tears in her eyes, his mother read aloud what she believed to be a glowing message: "Your son is a genius. This school is too small for him and doesn't have teachers who can properly train him. Please teach him yourself."

Years later, after his mother had passed away, Edison—by then one of the century's greatest inventors—found that same letter tucked away in a closet. Opening it, he discovered the truth: "Your son is mentally deficient. We cannot allow him to attend our school. He is expelled."

Edison reflected in his diary: "Thomas A. Edison was a mentally deficient child whose mother turned him into the genius of the century."

He had attended school for only a few months and had been partially deaf since childhood. Yet he was naturally curious, learning primarily through self-directed reading and experimentation. His mother recognized a potential far greater than what his teachers could see—a belief that ultimately helped Edison turn his talents into extraordinary achievements.

That's why the quote about potential is so powerful. If we truly did everything, we are capable of, we would astonish even ourselves. Yet, we can never know what we're truly capable of unless we take the first step and try.

Consider the story of Fauja Singh, a British Indian marathon runner. After the tragic deaths of his wife, son, and daughter, he moved to England to live with his remaining son. Remarkably, he began running at the age of 89. By 93, he had completed a marathon in 6 hours 54 minutes—almost an hour faster than the world record for his age group. That same year, 2004, he appeared in an Adidas campaign alongside icons like David Beckham and Muhammad Ali.

Fauja Singh could easily have withdrawn from life after enduring such profound losses. But he never gave up on a dream he had harboured since youth—a desire to run, which had been impossible due to poor health. Recognizing his potential, he began pursuing it at nearly 90. Within four years, he became a national sensation and a symbol of perseverance.

His story is proof that discovering and acting on your potential—even late in life—can transform everything. It's never too late to surprise the world, or yourself.

i) Power of Potential for Work.

Consider two bank executives, A and B, who join the same bank at the same time. A has been a branch manager for 10 years, performing the same role consistently. B, on the other hand, spent 4 years as a branch manager, then moved to wealth management for High-Net-Worth Individuals for 3 years, and later took on a treasury role at the corporate office for another 3 years. Both have the same total experience.

Who has the higher potential to grow and earn? Clearly, B does. Why? Because B sought out new challenges, adapted to different roles, and continuously pushed beyond comfort zones. Did B take career risks? Absolutely. But A's bigger risk was staying in the comfort zone. The greatest career risk is not taking any risk at all. If you never step out of your comfort zone, how will you learn, grow, or discover your true potential?

Career progression depends directly on your ability to adapt and deliver on challenging assignments. But how do you develop that ability? By gradually taking on increasingly complex roles as your career advances.

Thirty years ago, I was an area sales manager for a truck manufacturer in Madhya Pradesh—a region known for its gullies. Today, I am a global business leader covering Asia and Europe in an IT MNC. This transformation didn't happen overnight. I progressed step by step, taking on higher responsibilities every few years to test and expand my potential.

I was surprised to discover I could manage a country-level role in a completely different industry within just seven years of work. Fifteen years into my career, after multiple diverse roles, I stepped into a geo-level leadership position covering Asia Pacific and Japan.

Your career should evolve from a single-line specialization to T-shaped, then Pi-shaped, and eventually a comb-shaped trajectory. Imagine a comb: the handle represents your general management skills, while each tooth is a specialized expertise. I was fortunate to develop strong general management skills—people management, P&L, customer and partner management—while also gaining at least four "teeth" of specialization across e-commerce, PC business, services, India & APJ expertise, and sales & marketing. See the picture below.

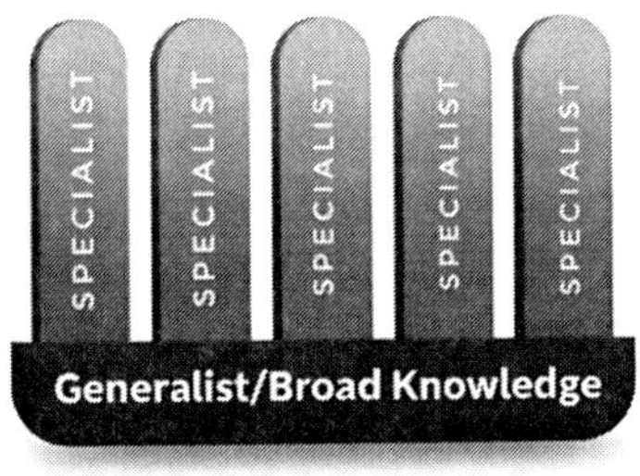

Comb Shaped Ideal Career, filled with multiple specialist skills and few generalist skills.

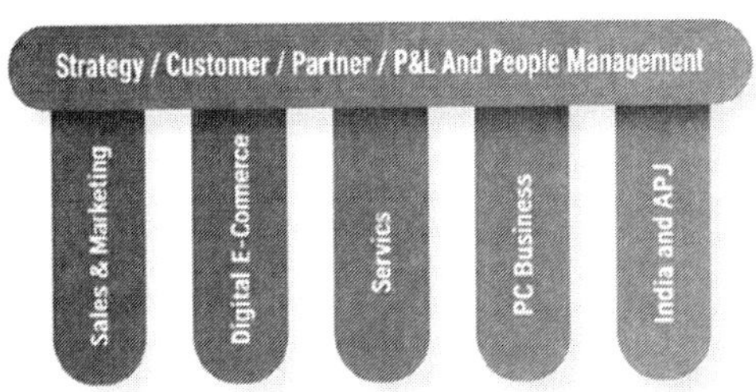

Nash "5 teeth" Career comb after 30 years of work.

How did I develop my potential and, consequently, my career? Any organization will have three axes for growth. Business unit,

Function and Geography, see picture below.

I took risks, and I moved across all three axes for both breadth & depth.

Business axis >> Printing >> Personal Systems >> Services BU

Function axis >> Channel Sales >> Marketing >> E-commerce sales

Geography axis >> Madhya Pradesh (Central/ West India) >> India >> Asia APJ >> Europe EMEA

Almost any organization will have these three axes in some form or another.

I would like to give example of two mentees of mine, who took my suggestion in this area and benefitted immensely. Their names have been changed to protect their privacy.

Shruti was a smart and hardworking girl, who spent more than 8 years in Marketing. She had stopped learning and was looking for a bigger role in marketing. When she sought my advice, I asked her if she ever considered sales as an option. She was quite hesitant at first. Then I gave examples of many women sales leaders who made a successful career, including our former HP India MD Neelam Dhawan and HP Global CEO Meg Whitman. I also explained to her the benefits of taking a variable compensation. Showing her how she can earn more by controlling her own destiny and results. Now after several years, when I see her as a successful salesperson, I feel very proud about her. She discovered her potential in sales, by taking that important first step of job change, using the functional axis.

Sachin was another mentee, who had done several roles within India organization. He was a currently a category manager, looking for a change and bigger responsibility. I asked him, if he was willing to explore an international, multi-country role. He was hesitant. Later when I showed him examples of others, including myself, who benefited from international exposure and learning opportunities, he was willing to make the move. I am very proud he is doing well in his new role, serving a different geography within the same company – an example of job change using the geo axis.

All these changes were not easy. It involved a few sessions explain the impact, pros and cons, the purpose and the easy steps you can take to make the leap. In the end, they realised, not taking any risk is the biggest risk.

Have you considered exploring these axes to advance your career?

Opportunities often come in confusing disguises. Mergers and acquisitions, for instance, are usually associated with job losses. Yet for talented individuals, they can open doors to promotions and larger roles. I've seen this happen three times in my career—during the DEC-Compaq merger, the Compaq-HP merger, and the EDS-HP merger. In these situations, while many focus inwardly on job security, true leaders focus outward—on customers and partners—ensuring their satisfaction and loyalty.

By taking extra initiative to grow the business, they attract attention, leading to greater responsibilities and the opportunity to realize their full potential.

In today's VUCA world—marked by Volatility, Uncertainty, Complexity, and Ambiguity—opportunities are everywhere. Competitors may become part of your company after a merger. Collaborators can turn into competitors with a shift in technology. Organizational structures and leadership change constantly. Yesterday's heroes and frameworks may be irrelevant today or tomorrow.

The key is not to lose sleep over these changes. Learn to embrace change and to act decisively amid ambiguity. Keep your focus external. Serve your customers even better when circumstances are uncertain. This approach not only ensures your team and company remain relevant but also allows you to perform at your highest potential, regardless of surrounding chaos.

ii) Power of Potential for Life.

How do you grow your potential in life? Be deliberate about your choices. Experiment, unless you try new things, you will not know what works for you. Also, treat life as an adventure. Don't get too bothered by ups and downs, which are part of life, but keep moving on.

The first tip to enhance your potential is to be deliberate in choosing your hobbies. In the earlier section on Passion, I suggested selecting three hobbies: one to stimulate curiosity (e.g., learning), one to develop a service orientation, and one to improve health. The key is not to choose randomly—take your time to select activities that align with your strengths, capabilities, and what truly brings you joy. When you are intentional, your potential will naturally grow.

Let me give you an example. For a health-related hobby, I could have returned to playing tennis, a sport I enjoyed in my youth. But I paused to analyse my situation. Our condominium had only two tennis courts, which were heavily booked, with only a handful of players available at any given time. Even if I had the time, the courts might be unavailable. I needed a daily exercise routine that I could perform consistently at my convenience.

I decided on brisk walking. Walking alone required no reservations, could be done at any time, and allowed me to listen to podcasts or catch up with friends and family. By choosing deliberately, I maintained consistency in my fitness routine while also enhancing my social interactions. This is a prime example of how thoughtful choices in hobbies can maximize your potential.

The second tip I would give is to experiment with different things in life. I have always loved singing and can perform decently in both English and Tamil. When one of my all-time favourite singers, SP Balasubrahmanyam, passed away, I was deeply moved. His melodious voice had been a constant companion throughout my childhood and youth—on the radio, on CDs, and later on my phone.

I learned that he had sung extensively in four languages: Hindi, Telugu, Kannada, and Tamil. I decided to create a private YouTube tribute for my friends and family, featuring seven of my favourite Tamil songs. But I didn't want to stop there. I realized that many of my friends spoke other languages, so I challenged myself to sing one song in each: Hindi, Kannada, and Telugu.

Initially, I was hesitant. Singing in languages I wasn't fluent in felt risky, but I gathered courage, practiced diligently, and recorded the songs. I combined these three tracks with my Tamil renditions and shared the video with my friends. Their appreciation and joy at hearing songs in their mother tongue delighted me.

Through this experience, I discovered hidden potential within myself—even beyond the age of 50 and in the wake of losing my favourite singer. The lesson: the best way to explore your potential is to experiment without fear, start safely among family and friends, and allow yourself to discover new abilities you never imagined.

The third tip I would give is not to take life too seriously and to treat it as an adventure. Have you ever watched small children at play? They notice a flower, a cat, or a bug with sheer wonder. They leap off cots, chairs, and tables without fear. Even if they fall and are injured, they cry, recover, and jump the next day. They don't dwell on failures, nor do they fear judgment. They approach life with curiosity and joy—a true sense of adventure.

Imagine if we could carry that childlike quality into our adult lives. Why are we so harsh and self-critical? Consider Steve Jobs, who was once fired from the very company he founded, or Donald Trump, who faced bankruptcy. How did they bounce back and achieve even greater success? I believe they embraced their failures with a sense of adventure, understanding that wins and losses are just part of life's game. Courage to keep moving forward is what matters most.

If you've read the latter memoir section about my motorcycle rides, you'll remember the most important lesson: treat the ride as an adventure. On a long ride, weather changes, road conditions shift and turns can hide the road just 100 meters ahead. Yet we don't let fear stop us—we ride carefully, adapt as needed, and enjoy the journey. Worrying too much about falls or punctures would prevent us from ever leaving the driveway. Life works the same way. We cannot foresee every challenge, but if we face it with an adventurous spirit, we can navigate the unknown with confidence.

By approaching life as an adventure, we open ourselves to experimentation, calculated risks, and new experiences. This mindset not only builds resilience but also dramatically enhances our potential, enabling us to embrace life fully, with courage and curiosity.

Practice time. Go to the later section, Applying Joyful Balance. Refer to Actionable Worksheet 2 – Meta Mind Six Step framework. For this area of Potential, think and jot down what you can apply in your work and life areas.

Chapter 11

PLANNING: DEVELOP REALISTIC & ACHIEVABLE SCHEDULES FOR LIFE & WORK.

"*Failing to plan is planning to fail*," Benjamin Franklin, a founding father of the USA.

Planning is the process of thinking about the activities required to achieve a desired goal. Planning is based on foresight, the fundamental capacity to think ahead, hence a key part of how human society evolves and progresses.

From historical times, greatest achievements of human beings have been made only by meticulous planning. I would give three examples.

1. First, the Indus Valley Civilization, dating back to 2500 BC, is notable for its planned grid layouts, sophisticated drainage

systems, and standardized brick sizes, indicating a high level of centralized planning, and it built some of the earliest cities in human history.

2. Second, Singapore's transformation from a small island nation to a global hub showcases meticulous urban planning, corruption-free government, and integration of economic development, green spaces, and technological advancements. I lived in Singapore for 5 years with my family, and I was always amazed by how this small nation achieved big results.
3. Third, the Apollo program, culminating in the first moon landing, was a monumental feat of planning, involving complex engineering, logistics, and a clear objective, overcoming significant technological hurdles and demonstrating human ingenuity to put a man on the moon and bring them safely back to earth.

i) Power of Planning for Work.

In work: A goal with a timeline helps. Compass Vs Clock. Learn, Contribute, Enjoy. Keep it simple.

A goal with a timeline helps. When you have a goal, even if it's not publicly stated, the universe conspires to make it happen. When I finished my MBA, "MD by 40" was my goal. Although not a Managing Director, I became a Marketing Director (MD) or APJ CMO at age 39. Smaller IT companies also offered to hire me as Managing Director. It is strange that at 22, when one finishes an MBA, one thinks one can conquer the world, unaware of the long journey ahead. Still having a goal at that stage with a timeline helps.

A promising career is a succession of increasingly challenging assignments or roles. A good role is like a tripod (see picture below), balanced on three legs, where you can learn, contribute, and enjoy all at the same time. If one of them is missing, it is time to consider a role change. Often, we become pretty comfortable with our jobs, typically after 3 years – it's not challenging enough anymore. Either you stop learning, are not contributing enough, or you feel bored. This is the time to seek a role change. Not all of us are lucky to get a new role ASAP, so it's good to plan, maybe a year in advance, with your manager.

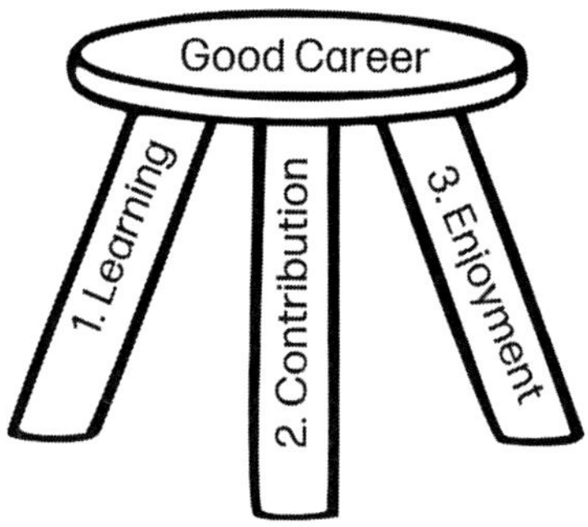

In the later section of my memoir, Gully to Global, you can see the different roles I played in the first decade of my work, 1991 to 2000. Every role gave me the opportunity to Learn, contribute, and enjoy. This plan allowed me to learn new things while contributing skills I already know. See the example below of my first few roles; you will get an idea of how to plan your career.

	Job	Responsibility	Learning	Contribution	Enjoyment
1	Area sales mgr. Eicher Mitsubishi Trucks for MP, Indore (1991-92)	. Revenue & Share . Customer mgmt. . Partner mgmt.	. Sales coverage . Line & Staff roles . Learnt Hindi	Exceeding revenue & market share goals for Madhya Pradesh territory	First job, first salary. Unfamiliar places, travel
2	Product Manager for Ford Cars & Trucks in Muscat, Oman (1992-95)	. Rev & Margin . Marketing . Inventory mgmt.	. US MNC in the Gulf . AS400 Computers . Demand/ Supply	Improved sales and reduced inventory (computerization)	Ford, the Auto world leader. Working abroad. Got a car when I was 25 years old
3	Product Mgr. for HP Printers in HCL-HP in Noida (1996-97)	. Rev & Margin . Market share . Channel mgmt.	. US-India JV . IT Products . Brand Mgmt.	Improved share for HP Printers in India, in Home and Office	HCL India's No.1 IT brand. Working in NCR of India

4	Product Mgr. for PCs in HP (Compaq) India, Bengaluru (1997-2000)	. Rev & Margin . Market share . Product Life Cycle	. 4P's PLC mgmt. . Opex mgmt. . Marketing mgmt.	Made HP (Compaq) India's No.1 Business PS Brand, beating HCL (1999)	HP World's No.1 Brand, Bengaluru, Tech Capital

I could not have moved from area sales manager for trucks in the auto industry to national product manager for computers in the IT industry, in one move. I moved from one role to the next, leveraging my experience. Eicher to Ford, using Auto experience. Ford to HCL using Product Mgmt. experience. HCL to HP/Compaq using IT experience.

That is the power of planning in your career. "To remain static is to lose ground," said HP founder David Packard. It's true in your career too. PLAN and pursue new roles with the same passion as the day you took your first job, like a child with curiosity to learn about the wide world.

ii) Compass vs Clock

Another important consideration in planning your career is knowing when to slow down and take on strategic roles. This helps you build a different set of skills—a sort of "compass versus clock" mindset.

Between 1998 and 2000, I was the Commercial PC Category Manager for Compaq India, the world's No.1 PC brand at the time. I was swamped, averaging 12 hours a day on weekdays and another six on Saturdays—around 60 hours a week in a pre-smartphone era! Our category management team was lean, almost like a startup. I served in multiple roles: product manager, marketing manager, channel training manager, and pricing strategist—essentially managing all four Ps for the brand.

The toughest part was balancing opposite demands: negotiating transactional price clearances for bids one moment, shaping product strategy for India with HQ in Houston a year in advance the next, and visiting Fortune 50 enterprise customers one day, conducting channel training in small towns the next. My workdays usually began at 8:30 a.m. and ended around 9:30 p.m. If I returned by 7 p.m., my wife would joke, "Is today a half-day at the office?" Month-ends were even longer; I once came home at 1 a.m. My wife had gone to sleep after getting our daughter ready for school, but my mother cheerfully greeted me: "Good morning! Dinner is ready on the table!" Only when you come home after midnight can someone truly say, "Good morning, dinner is ready." 😊

After 3 years in such a demanding role, I had the opportunity to establish India's first online PC store in 2000. When I took on that role, for the first time I had no one calling me or writing to me for a week. I felt so unwanted suddenly. One quote from a Compaq VP (an Australian named Paul Blinkhorn) then gave me hope. He said, when you do an important job, like launching a new online store, the compass (direction) is more important than the clock (speed). He taught me to appreciate the value of NOT being busy to do important work. With this immortal quote from Nobel Laureate Prof James Watson (of DNA double helix fame) "It's necessary to be slightly underemployed if you are to do something significant."

In 1999, Compaq (later acquired by HP) surpassed HCL in commercial PC shipments, becoming the No. 1 Commercial PC brand for the first time. In 2000, Compaq launched India's first online store for PCs, which also became India's largest e-commerce site by revenue (ahead of Rediff.com and Sify.com). One job kept me busy. Another job required me to be strategic. I learnt the value of being NOT busy and underemployed for a while and doing something significant. Not everyone gets that privilege. Eternally grateful to all my leaders who gave me these opportunities in HP🙏

US President Eisenhower, a man who commanded one of the most complex military operations in history, said, "Plans are nothing; planning is everything." He understood that a plan is a static document, but planning is a dynamic process. Likewise, ask yourself this question if you are very busy in your career. What is the next role I can plan for myself, which will make me more strategic and develop different skill sets inside my brain? Keep refining your career plans but always plan.

iii) Power of Planning for Life.

Just like work, in life too, you can put the power of planning to work. We saw earlier how a career is just one part of life. Balance is key. We need to focus on multiple areas in life and put a balanced plan. In wealth management, we don't put all eggs in one basket. We diversify with a Portfolio approach (Mutual funds, Gold, Stocks, and Real Estate). Likewise, you need a portfolio approach to build your career and life by doing different things at the same time, rather than focusing on a single profession.

Allow me to introduce the concept of Portfolio life. A "portfolio life" refers to a way of living and working in which individuals engage in multiple, diverse activities and careers simultaneously, rather than focusing on a single traditional career path. This approach, first coined by Charles Handy, emphasizes a more fulfilling and well-rounded life by integrating personal passions, interests, and skills with financial stability. It's about actively curating a life that reflects a variety of experiences, rather than being defined by a singular job title or career trajectory.

There is a nice book called "Portfolio Life" written by Prof. Christina Wallace (Author) from Harvard Business School, where she says, and I reproduce, "You are more than your job. Pouring yourself into a single full-time job is the riskiest move you can make. Your parents' advice to focus on one career path? It no longer works for reasons ranging from recessions to student loan debt, the gig economy, climate disasters, and a global pandemic, to name a few. We need a dramatically different relationship with work, one that allows us to define ourselves beyond our paid labour. The answer? A Portfolio Life. An anti-hustle, pro-rest approach to work-life balance, a Portfolio Life is built on three tenets, a Portfolio Life: 1. You are more than any one role or opportunity. 2. Diversification will help you navigate change and mitigate uncertainty. 3. When (not if) your needs change, you can and should rebalance."

Even before I learnt about this book and its core concepts, I had been developing my life plan, integrating various aspects of my life. This aligns with the widely used portfolio life concept. I said what the six things are that are important to me. It was career, health, financial wealth, relationships with family and friends, happiness, and caring for others. I started planning and set goals in all these areas to achieve a joyful balance in life.

iv) Balanced goals

	Area	**Perpetual Goal (Example)**	**Specific goal and Key action steps (Example)**
1	Health	Stay fit and active till the last day I live	Yoga and Meditation – 30 min/ day. Brisk walking – 30 min/day. Engage a fitness trainer and a dieting coach
2	Happiness	Do activities that give me joy	Long rides on Motorcycles every quarter. Photography. Karaoke singing. Writing books/ blogs. Happiness coach.
3	Career	Drive for excellence in every role I perform	Increase revenue, margin, and customer satisfaction for every business I lead.
4	Care	Serve others with hands, head, heart, and wallet	Sathya Saibaba seva activities. Teaching E-com at B-school. Leadership & happiness coaching for young professionals.
5	Family	Have cordial relationships with Family and Friends	Weekly calls with close relatives, monthly calls with close friends, in person meetings whenever a good friend visits my town.
6	Financial	Financial independence to take care of my family.	Financial plan to retire by age 50. Monthly SIP now to SWP later. Term and medical insurance.

My portfolio life comprises many roles in addition to my corporate employment. I am a teacher, coach, mentor, biker, writer, photographer, and family man. This way, I am quite diversified and have a sense of joyful balance. It all started with planning. The plan I developed in 2015 continues to be refined. But the process of planning remains essential.

Practice time. Go to the later section, Applying Joyful Balance. Refer to Actionable Worksheet 2 – Meta Mind Six Step framework. For this area of Planning, think and jot down what you can apply in your work and life areas.

Chapter 12

PEOPLE: - POWER OF FRIENDS, FAMILY, MENTORS & COMMUNITY

"75 percent of long-term job success depends on people skills, while only 25 percent on technical knowledge." Peggy Klaus, author of the bestselling book, The Hard Truth About Soft Skills

People skills, also known as interpersonal skills, are the abilities that enable cordial and effective interaction with others. These skills are essential to success in both work and life, fostering better relationships, teamwork, and communication to achieve outcomes. They encompass a range of competencies, such as empathy, active listening, clarity of communication, and conflict resolution.

Several notable figures are celebrated for their exceptional interpersonal skills. Mahatma Gandhi, leader of the Indian independence movement, exemplified excellent communication and empathy. He was not the governor general, nor held any official government post, but when he spoke, half a billion people listened. He had the unique ability to lead with truth, justice, and non-violence as his weapons. His refusal to pay tax to the British colonial government on common salt was communicated to the people without a word, conveyed through his walking to Dandi Beach with his millions of followers and making salt there. He spoke in simplicity, without uttering a single word, just by his actions of giving up his barrister-type fine suits and wearing the simple white cloth worn by most Indians. He could unite people of all religions, castes, and creeds with his powerful vision for an independent India, free from the colonial yoke. In the contemporary era, Oprah Winfrey is often cited as a prime example of her exceptional people skills. Her ability to connect with people stems from her empathy, genuine interest in others, and powerful communication skills. She fosters a sense of trust and relatability, making people feel heard and understood. Her openness and vulnerability, coupled with her ability to ask insightful questions, create a strong emotional connection with her audience.

i) Power of People for Work.

Tip 1: Understand your role, to determine better, the people skills required.

At work, people skills will vary, depending on your role in the organisation. If you are an individual contributor (IC) and starting in your career, you will spend a lot of time focused on specialized tasks and executing projects that your manager expects from you. Later, when you transition to a management role, you will guide your people to get things done. Lastly, if you become a leader, your focus is on strategic vision and overall organizational success. You will see that many leaders can influence people without formal authority, including those beyond your company in the industry. Transitioning between these roles often involves developing new skills and adapting to different priorities.

		Example	Responsibilities	Skills required	Career growth comes by
1	Individual Contributor	Marketing specialist or Area Sales rep	Executing tasks, meeting deadlines, and achieving goals	Technical expertise, problem-solving, and time management	Overseeing more complex projects (breadth) or developing specialized skills (depth).
2	Manager	Marketing or Sales manager	Setting goals, delegating tasks, providing feedback.	People management, communication, delegation, and conflict resolution.	Managing larger teams, taking on more strategic responsibilities.
3	Leader	The CEO or Director sets the company's direction and guides multiple teams.	Strategic planning, communicating the vision, and building stakeholder relationships.	Visionary thinking, strategic planning, communication, and influencing.	Can progress by influencing the broader organization or driving meaningful change.

I would take three jobs, as I did, to illustrate how I performed these roles and the people skills required.

		Responsibilities	**Skills required**
1	Product manager for the Compaq PC business in India (Individual Contributor role)	Revenue, Margin, Market share. Executing tasks like new product launches, channel trainings, supply/ demand planning, and marketing execution	Technical expertise in product management, time management, critical thinking skills, and a cordial collaborative nature for collaborating with people
2	Technology Services GM for HP in India (Manager role)	Revenue, Margin, Customer satisfaction. Led a team of fifty people, tech consultants with four managers. Understanding Customer requirements, Project mgmt., setting goals, executing by delegating tasks.	Empathy, Customer handling skills, People management, providing feedback, communication, and delegation, resolving conflicts.

3	Head of Digital Business for HP India (Leader role)	Build a digital platform to cover six hundred physical stores in three hundred cities. Build shared capabilities for Digital Marketing, Analytics, KYC, and CRM for multiple partner companies. Prepare them to compete with Amazon and similar firms. Strategic planning, communicating the vision, building stakeholder consent relationships, and execution.	Strategy and planning skills, Technology services skills, vendor and partner management skills, project management skills, Visionary thinking, strategic planning, communication, and influencing people without directly managing anyone, and building stakeholder consent and execution.

All the above roles required people skills. However, as I became more senior, the breadth and depth of these people skills became more sophisticated. From executing tasks to managing people to leading teams that don't even report to you, it is a change we need to make, as we build our careers.

Tip 2: Network is your net worth.

Many times, even if you are fully capable of doing a role, you might not get selected for the role. Why? There are many candidates just like you who are as good as you. There are plenty of choices for a recruiter. What differentiates you is not only what you know but also who you know. And who knows you? Let me elaborate.

What you know = Technical expertise, if you can get the job done.

Who you know = Your circle of friends, current and ex-colleagues, acquaintances, etc.

Who knows you? Do you have the character and reputation at work to be known by senior people in the industry?

Both character and reputation are important, but they are distinct. Character refers to your inner values, while reputation is how others perceive you based on your actions and behaviours. While character is about who you truly are, reputation is what people think you are. A good reputation can be built on a strong character. But that requires some effort in personal brand building.

1) Respect everyone, be cordial in every relationship. Ego and Anger are a BIG NO.
2) Network strategically: Connect with people in your industry and build relationships.
3) Have no-agenda relationships, where there is no expectation from others, except for their company.

4) Seek feedback. Ask for input on your work and identify areas for improvement.
5) Be authentic. Let your personality shine through and be genuine in your interactions.
6) Stand for something and stay true to your values.
7) Don't be shy to talk about your good work. People must attest to your credibility even when you are not present.

Tip 3: Good managers are great role models.

If you observe your seniors and managers, you can learn many valuable people skills. You can even model a few of the good behaviours they possess. I have had more than 20 direct and dotted managers in my life. A few were exceptionally good, great managers and mentors. I learnt a great deal from them about business management, strategy, and execution. I have covered that in a separate section at the beginning of this book. However, in this section, I would like to highlight a few points I learned from them and implemented for myself.

1. MBWA – Management by walking around. This was a core principle of our founders, Bill Hewlett and Dave Packard. This is simply walking up to your colleague's desk every week and checking whether everything is okay. Learned from Rajiv Srivastava.
2. Show up when it matters. When your colleagues are going through important career phases, just showing up and being there with them sends a very positive signal. I learned from Som Mittal.

3. Rule of 5 emails - If you are having a conversation on email and have written more than 5 emails on the same subject, stop writing emails. Organize a short call or F2F meeting and thrash things out. This can quickly close many open issues. Learned from Scott Basford.
4. Rule of Four people meal. As we rise within a company, people tend to form their own empires, and egos come in inadvertently. For making important decisions with senior people, limit the face-to-face meeting to three or four people who can sit around a table for a meal. Most of the work will be completed in one sitting over a meal, as learned from Jean Paul Wagner.
5. Trust and respect – if you have given someone a job, let them do it. Do not micromanage and ask for status frequently. You need to respect the individual's capabilities and trust them to do the job. Learned from Michelle Weiss.

What people skills did you learn from your own seniors and managers?

ii) Power of People for Life.

Gurus, mentors, relatives, and friends play a significant role in shaping one's life. Which friend do you remember after many years – the Ivy League consultant, OR the friend who helped you when it mattered? When you look back at life, people remember your small acts of kindness better than your profound ideas. After many years in the hardware industry, I learned about a new services position. This happened over a cup of coffee while chatting with an old colleague whom I had not seen in many years. Being nice helped me personally. Being nice every day is the fastest way to get work done. As the saying goes, "It is nice to be important, but it is more important to be nice".

A few conversations I have had with a few of my friends have fundamentally altered my worldview on many things.

1. "What have you done for the world, apart from feeding yourself and family?" On one of my birthdays, a friend casually asked me the question. He had undertaken numerous service activities throughout his life, in addition to being a successful corporate employee. This single question prompted me to reflect deeply on my life. Within a year, I joined the Sathya Sai Seva organization and spent at least a few hours per month serving food to older adults, people with disabilities, the homeless, and those in need. This made me a better human being. Thanks, Sai Chandrasekar.
2. "Do you know the difference between reaction and response?" I argued with someone, and one of my friends was observing this from a distance. After I calmed down, he approached me and asked me this question. He said, I reacted to the situation (emotionally) rather than responding (logically). That conversation taught me the importance of mastering your mind. This made me a calmer person. Thanks, Rama Tadepalli.
3. "You will fall from your bike, but you have to pick yourself up, drink some water, and continue to ride." This was a tip from my motorbike captain and rider, Balaji Devanathan, when I went on my first Himalayan ride with him. After that,

I did two more Himalayan rides with him. My fear of failure vanished after that.

4. "Service can be a positive wish or even a prayer". During a conversation, my 90+ year-old mother, Jaya Govindarajan, mentioned this line. I always associated service to others only with hands, heads, or a wallet. She bought another dimension of pure love with her heart. She talked about how she prays every day for her close relatives, including me, wishing for positive things in my life, good health, prosperity, and a long life. And that is service. This led me to consider how we can serve others, even in old age; what matters is love and intention.
5. "You achieved a lot at a young age," my life companion and my wife of close to 30 years, Padmapriya, said this line once, when I had a difficult time at work. She advised me to be happy and content, and not always long for more, because I achieved a lot at a young age. That was true, but it required someone else to observe and inform me, as I was blind to it. This made me a more content person.
6. "Ask what you want, not what you don't want, as the mind cannot process a double negative well." This was a neuro-linguistic programming (NLP) technique taught by a coach, Adam Khoo, in Singapore, which changed my life. For example, instead of saying "I want to lose weight," say what you want to do: "I want to get fit, eat right, and exercise every day". That's why our elders always say, shubh shubh bolo (Say only good things).
7. Power of affirmations. Learned from Meta Mind international coaches Varsha and Avinash Ananda. If you want to achieve

something in life, say affirmations in the personal, positive, and present tense. "I am a successful book author now." It's personal, positive, and in the present tense, even though I have yet to publish a book 😊. It worked for other things; it will work for this, too.

What have you learnt from your relatives, close friends, and mentors that has made you a better person?

Practice time. Go to the later section, Applying Joyful Balance. Refer to Actionable Worksheet 2 – Meta Mind Six Step framework. For this area of People, think and jot down what you can apply in your work and life areas.

Chapter 13

PERSISTENCE: MAINTAIN YOUR COURSE DESPITE SETBACKS AND CHANGES.

"Persistence can change failure into extraordinary achievement," Matt Biondi, world champion swimmer and Eight-time Olympic Gold medal winner.

Persistence is the continued effort to do something even when it's difficult or when you face obstacles. It's about not giving up and staying determined to achieve a goal. There have been countless humans in history who faced challenges but persevered. People like Nelson Mandela, Steve Jobs, J.K. Rowling, and APJ Abdul Kalam harnessed the potential of their minds while enduring numerous struggles. They kept moving forward, raising the bar each time.

The person who has inspired me most regarding persistence is Arunima Sinha. She once spoke at a company event, and within 30 minutes, everyone in the room, including me, was moved to tears. Her story of resilience is nothing short of extraordinary.

Arunima Sinha is the first female amputee in the world to scale Mount Everest—a true embodiment of grit and fortitude. Before her mountaineering journey, she was part of the Indian national volleyball team. In 2011, while traveling by train, she was attacked by robbers who tried to steal her belongings. When she resisted, they threw her from the moving train, leaving her with severe injuries, including a broken spine and a crushed leg that ultimately led to amputation.

For many, such a setback would have been insurmountable. But Arunima decided to transform her tragedy into a mission: to climb Mount Everest. She pushed herself through gruelling rehabilitation, learning to walk with a prosthetic limb while simultaneously preparing for the extreme demands of mountaineering. Under the mentorship of Bachendri Pal, the first Indian woman to climb Everest, Arunima trained relentlessly, pushing past limits, enduring pain, and never losing sight of her goal.

On May 21, 2013, she reached the summit of Mount Everest, becoming the first female amputee to do so. Her journey didn't stop there. Driven by passion and unwavering persistence, she went on to conquer five more of the world's highest peaks: Kilimanjaro in Africa, Elbrus in Europe, Kosciuszko in Australia, Aconcagua in Argentina, and Carstensz Pyramid in Indonesia.

Arunima Sinha's story is living proof that the human spirit, fuelled by persistence and courage, can overcome adversity and accomplish even the seemingly impossible.

i) Power of persistence for work:

Let us see how to harness the power of persistence at work.

Tip 1. Start with simple goals.

Often at work, we scatter our energies across too many tasks, diluting our focus. There is immense power in focus—channelling it on the most important tasks yields far greater results. Learn to identify your highest-priority work and commit to completing it.

If you are a manager, it's critical to clearly communicate expectations to your team. If you are a leader managing other managers, simplicity becomes even more important. I once had a manager leading a 1,000+ person organization in a complex, matrixed structure. Each person had different goals, and many didn't even report directly to him. Yet he found a brilliant way to unify everyone with a 9-word goal sheet:

"Meet your numbers. Satisfy your customers. Grow your people."

In just nine words, he captured the essence of everyone's responsibilities. Each person had a number—revenue, margin, or operational efficiency. Every individual had a customer—internal or external—who was tracked through NPS (Net Promoter Score). Each team member was responsible for developing their own skills and growth.

This simple, clear framework aligned everyone's efforts and made persistence toward achieving goals not just possible, but inevitable.

Tip 2. Take on challenging assignments and deliver results in tough times.

The way to strengthen your persistence muscle is to take on assignments that truly test it. As the saying goes, when the going gets tough, the tough get going. In my career, I faced multiple adversities: three mega-mergers (Digital, Compaq, EDS), frequent internal reorganizations that put my job at risk, and unforeseen macroeconomic shocks—the 2000 dot-com crash, the 2007 financial meltdown, and the 2020 COVID-19 disruptions.

Each challenge was an opportunity to take on difficult assignments and deliver. I built Compaq India's online store in 2000 amid the dot-com crash, led HP India's Technology Services business to become the fastest-growing in the world in 2007 during the Lehman collapse, and delivered record e-commerce quarters in 2020 despite COVID-19-related supply chain disruptions. Looking back, these experiences dramatically strengthened my resilience.

Think of it this way—would we celebrate Arunima Sinha, the Paralympic mountaineer, for her grit if she hadn't faced and overcome unimaginable adversity? True persistence is forged in the most challenging times.

Tip 3. Your past milestones must motivate you.

Much of how we feel and act in life depends on perspective. You can see the glass as half-full or half-empty. I set an early goal—to build a solid career in the IT industry. Along the way, I saw friends and colleagues reach heights I never did. I could have felt demoralized, asking, "Why not me?" Instead, I focused on my own milestones and kept persisting.

Milestone 1: After spending the first five years in the automotive industry without an electronics background, I became a country product manager at one of India's top IT companies—before turning 30.

Milestone 2: I became a manager of managers (Director) even before turning 40. I may not have risen as fast as Satya Nadella at Microsoft or Sundar Pichai at Google to become CEO, but reflecting on my own journey and achievements gave me the strength to pursue bigger goals.

When you feel down, look back at how far you've come. When pride clouds your judgment, look ahead at where you still need to go. Balancing these two perspectives gives you the power to persist and overcome the odds in your career.

Tip 4: No substitute for Hard work.

There is no substitute for old-fashioned hard work and performance, even in the new world. Often, people with Ivy League educations are passed over in Favor of those who deliver better results. Proactivity, coupled with good planning, excellent teamwork, and execution, yields strong performance. When you deliver results, people sit up and take notice, whether you speak well or not. A colleague once said, one can never look good with bad numbers. Nor can it look bad with good numbers. Persist and put in the hard work. Results will come in one day.

I would like to give an example of a mentee, Gagan*, who was a brilliant computer scientist, who was an expert in the area of machine learning. He was serving the USA market out of India. He went through a very difficult time, as he had a misunderstanding with his manager, which only worsened over time. Despite his being a key player, his manager sidelined him and started giving more opportunities to lesser qualified people. He came to me for advice. I coached him for a few sessions. Asked him to start with simple goals which motivate him. Then focus of learning the latest and being the best in his field, ignoring all the nonsense happening around him. He put his best work despite the odds. He did not let his managers attitude affect him. I also told him to look for opportunities outside his immediate organization where he can showcase his talent. In a matter of 6 months, the opportunity came and he was selected for a different role with much higher pay. I am very proud of his capability to focus on his work and upgrade himself, despite the organisational odds. It's an example of persistence paying. * Mentees name changed to protect the privacy.

ii) Power of persistence for life:

Let us see how to leverage the power of persistence in life.

Tip 1: Know everyone has problems.

Think of rich people, who have all the wealth and power. Elon Musk, Jeff Bezos, Mukesh Ambani, or Jack Ma. Think of entertainers who have all the fame. Brad Pitt, Jackie Chan, Shah Rukh Khan, Taylor Swift, or AR Rahman. Think of all sportspersons who won ultimate glory for their countries with Olympic Gold medals or winning the World Cup, like Usain Bolt, Lionel Messi, or Virat Kohli. Do you think these people with all their power, wealth, and fame will have no problems in life? Not at all. The larger the personality, the more problems they have overcome. Everyone has problems. It is their capacity to persist in doing their work despite the odds that truly separates them from others. Read the biographical account of every one of them. None of them had it easy in life. So, accept the fact, persist, and keep working.

Tip 2: Attitude of gratitude

The legendary Wimbledon champion Arthur Ashe contracted AIDS from a contaminated blood transfusion during heart surgery in 1983. While battling the illness, he received a letter from a fan asking, “Why did God choose you, such a good person, for such a terrible disease?” Ashe’s reply was remarkable:

“Fifty million children started playing tennis, five million learned the game, 500,000 became professional players, 50,000 entered the circuit, 5,000 reached Grand Slam tournaments, 50 reached Wimbledon, four reached the semifinals, two reached the finals—and when I was holding the cup in my hand, I never asked God, ‘Why me?’ So now, in pain, how can I ask God, ‘Why me?’”

What a profoundly spiritual perspective. Ashe undoubtedly felt physical pain, yet he never suffered mentally. Pain is physical; suffering is mental. Like Arunima Sinha or Arthur Ashe, these individuals embody grit, persistence, and resilience by maintaining an attitude of gratitude even in the face of adversity.

It's easy to forget the many blessings in life when challenges arise in career or personal life. That's exactly when counting your blessings matters most. If you are reading this and able to reflect, you are already ahead of millions who cannot read—or worse, cannot pause to think. An attitude of gratitude shapes your persistence, builds resilience, and determines your altitude in life.

Tip 3: Spirituality and Service

Many people, focused on material success, struggle to grasp the essence of spirituality. At its core, spirituality is the search for meaning, purpose, and a connection to something larger than oneself. It may involve belief in a higher power, a bond with nature, or a sense of interconnectedness with humanity and the universe. If that feels abstract, think of spirituality simply as selfless service to humanity. By serving others without expecting anything in return, you cultivate empathy, humility, and a deep, lasting joy that comes from contributing to the well-being of those around you.

There's a saying: "There is never a traffic jam on the extra mile." It means that those who go beyond the call of duty face less competition, discover more opportunities, and enjoy greater rewards. I've witnessed this principle in action multiple times throughout my life. When selfless service becomes a habit, the returns—both tangible and intangible—are immense.

Why bring this up under resilience? Life often seems unfair. The deserving may be overlooked for promotions, the meek may be bullied by the strong, and selfish individuals may appear to thrive. But they are mistaken—there is a higher order at work. Call it God, Nature, the Universe, or even your favourite hero—Superman or Wonder Woman. They will face the consequences of their actions; they reap what they sow. Your responsibility is your own karma. Focus on your work, remain steadfast in the face of challenges, serve others selflessly, and nurture your resilience. Struggle is the precursor to success, and persistence ensures that, when victory comes, it is deeply meaningful.

Practice time. Go to the later section, Applying Joyful Balance. Refer to Actionable Worksheet 2 – Meta Mind Six-Step framework. For this area of Persistence, think and jot down what you can apply in your work and life areas.

PART 4

STEPS TO APPLY THIS BOOK'S LEARNINGS NOW.

Chapter 14

ACTIONABLE WORKSHEETS TO BRING JOYFUL BALANCE TO DAILY LIFE

Let us briefly review what we have learnt so far. In Part 1, we did three things. We examined the myths and misconceptions surrounding work-life balance, success, and happiness. We then examined what is preventing us from achieving the desired outcomes. We then understood the megatrends shaping our future and how to identify opportunities in a VUCA environment. In Part 2, we covered how to avoid negativity and focus on the ten foundational beliefs that empower you. In Part 3, we introduced the Meta Mind Six Step Framework for Joyful Balance, namely - Purpose, Passion, Potential, Planning, People, and Persistence, with examples of how this can be applied at work and in life.

In this part, I'll explain how to put all these learnings into an action plan. I prefer to keep this section relatively simple, focusing on principles rather than complex templates. This way, you build your own action plan in a style that suits you. The action plan consists of just three things. First, examining the applicability of foundational beliefs, second, reflecting on what will work on the six-step framework for you, and third, defining success on your terms. I have given you three actionable worksheets, which you can either fill out in this book or on a photocopy of this page on a separate sheet of paper. Take your time to do it, preferably in the morning after a good night's rest, when you are in a relaxed state of mind. Revisit the filled-up sheet after a few days to refine it.

In the next parts, I give a better context for my learning through my memoir. We read about my personal transformation story from burnout to breakthrough, through the power of Joyful Balance. Then my career story from Gully to Global as a corporate employee, the importance of learning from great leaders, the importance of hobbies, my learnings as a motorcycle rider, the Importance of giving back, and my experience as a teacher.

My Actionable Worksheet 1 – Empowering Beliefs.

Examine and eliminate negative and apply empowering beliefs:

Examine and remove any negative self-beliefs that are harming you. Use the empowering beliefs from my list below, then adapt them in your work and life. You can think along the lines of "Stop, Start, and Continue". What can I stop doing that is harming my journey to Joyful Balance? What must I start doing, and what can I continue doing, to achieve a joyfully balanced life of Happiness and Success in Work and Life?

1. Define your unique success path. Never compare.
   How to adapt in my Work (Career)?

•
•
•
•
•

How to adapt in my Life (Outside work)?

•
•
•
•
•

2. Happiness fuels success, not the other way around. Satisfaction beats success.
   How to adapt in my Work (Career)?

•
•
•
•

How to adapt in my Life (Outside work)?

•
•
•
•

3. Reframe every challenge as an opportunity or adventure.
   How to adapt in my Work (Career)?

-
-
-
-

   How to adapt in my Life (Outside work)?

-
-
-
-
-

4. Think positive, dream big, and convert negative self-talk to positive.
   How to adapt in my Work (Career)?

-
-
-
-
-

   How to adapt in my Life (Outside work)?

-
-
-
-
-

5. The best investment is in oneself, learning meta skills.
   How to adapt in my Work (Career)?

.
.
.
.
.

How to adapt in my Life (Outside work)?

.
.
.
.
.

6. Work-life balance pyramid or radar chart.
   How to adapt in my Work (Career)?

.
.
.
.
.

How to adapt in my Life (Outside work)?

.
.
.
.
.

7. Collecting the Gold coins (not just silver coins) in life
   How to adapt in my Work (Career)?

-
-
-
-
-

How to adapt in my Life (Outside work)?

-
-
-
-
-

8. Hard work and action speak louder than words.
   How to adapt in my Work (Career)?

-
-
-
-
-

How to adapt in my Life (Outside work)?

-
-
-
-
-

9. Acceptance, not getting what you want, is also good luck.
   How to adapt in my Work (Career)?

-
-
-
-

   How to adapt in my Life (Outside work)?

-
-
-
-

10. Good Karma, reap as you sow, the giver's mindset.
    How to adapt in my Work (Career)?

-
-
-
-

    How to adapt in my Life (Outside work)?

-
-
-
-

My Actionable Worksheet 2 – Meta Mind Six Step Framework.

Examine and apply the Meta Mind Six Step Framework for Joyful Balance below. Think about what you can adapt as your work and life goals and actions. Look at the table below, pick out a few points that apply to you, and write an action list.

	Six Step Framework	Work	Life
1	Purpose: Rediscover your WHY.	Purpose powers career. Join great teams with big goals.	Life beyond work is key. Develop an abundance mindset.
2	Passion: What energizes & fulfils you?	Do a job you love. Learn first, earn next.	Keep Learning. Choose hobbies to grow CASH, Curiosity, Acceptance, Service, Health.
3	Potential: Exploit your strengths.	Take risks, move for breadth & depth. Ride through VUCA	Experiment. Treat life as an adventure.
4	Planning: Build realistic plans.	Have a goal with a timeline. Plan to Learn, Contribute, Enjoy	Live a Portfolio life.
5	People: Power of Friends & Family	Build your Network. Learn from good managers.	Power of being nice and doing good Have Life conversations with friends.
6	Persistence: Stay on track through setbacks.	Stick to a simple plan, stay focused. Reflect on milestones that motivate.	Develop an attitude of gratitude. Focus on Service and Spirituality

1. Purpose: Rediscover your WHY.
   How to adapt in my Work (Career)?

.

.

.

.

How to adapt in my Life (Outside work)?

.

.

.

.

2. Passion: What energizes & fulfils you.
   How to adapt in my Work (Career)?

.

.

.

.

How to adapt in my Life (Outside work)?

.

.

.

.

3. Potential: Exploit your strengths.
   How to adapt in my Work (Career)?

.

.

.

.

How to adapt in my Life (Outside work)?

-
-
-
-

4. Planning: Build realistic plans.

   How to adapt in my Work (Career)?

-
-
-
-

How to adapt in my Life (Outside work)?

-
-
-
-

5. People: Power of Friends & Family

   How to adapt in my Work (Career)?

-
-
-
-

How to adapt in my Life (Outside work)?

-
-
-
-

6. Persistence: Stay on track through setbacks.

   How to adapt in my Work (Career)?

-
-
-
-
-

   How to adapt in my Life (Outside work)?

-
-
-
-
-

My Actionable Worksheet 3 – Define your unique success plan:

Define what success is to you. Reject societal definitions of success & write your own success plan. Your unique path, based on your life circumstances. The 5 or 6 things you want to accomplish in life in the next 10 years. This must be a well-balanced plan covering major area of life, beyond work as well. Next, list a few actions you will take daily or weekly to achieve the above goals. For health and wealth goals, I would suggest working with specialists such as Certified Financial Planners, Dietitians, and Fitness trainers. For other goals, you can take ideas from my six-step framework. Why? Refer to the appendix for my accomplishments in these areas and my unique expertise in writing this book. If you finish points 1, 2, and 3, your unique success plan for joyful balance will look like this.

	Area	Goal (Sample)	Key action steps (Sample)
1	Health	Stay fit and active. Eat right. Hit XX weight by XX date.	Consult a fitness trainer or join a GYM. Consult a Dietitian. Join Yoga and Meditation classes.
2	Wealth	Financially independent by XX age, taking care of duties towards family	Consult a Certified Financial Planner (CFP) and audit for expenses, savings, insurance, and plan for your life goals.
3	Social	Spend more time with family.	I will spend 15 minutes with my family at home daily. Weekly activity. Refer to the Beliefs and Six-P framework for more ideas.
4	Happiness	Do activities that give me joy	Motorcycle riding. Learn Painting, Guitar, or Photography. Refer to the Six-P framework for more ideas.
5	Career	Drive for role excellence.	Exceed my numbers, targets. Join XYZ courses to upskill myself. Refer to the Six-P framework for more ideas.

My goals above are mostly non-numeric and timeless. You can also set goals that are numeric. Example: For wealth, build a net worth of XX Lakhs or Crores. For health, run 10 km in under 1 hour. For my Career, I aim to become an MD by age 40 at a mid-sized company. Or start a company before turning 35 years, etc. Finish an E-MBA program from a top-tier institution by year 20XX. See the next page for the Unique Success Plan template.

My unique success plan:

	Area	My Goal	My every week/day action steps
1	Health	. . . . .	. . . . .
2	Wealth	. . . . .	. . . . .
3	Social	. . . . .	. . . . .

4	Happiness	. . . . .	. . . . .
5	Career	. . . . .	. . . . .

A few other tips.

1. Once you define your success plan, start acting on it. Track your actions Vs plans.
2. Be mindful. Begin observing your own life as if you were a third person.
3. Develop a daily ritual of habits. Example: every morning or evening, go for a walk.
4. Periodically, refine your plans if assumptions change.
5. Persist, and you will attain a joyful balance.

When you live joyfully balanced lives, you will:

1. Perform better at work, happier.
2. Become role models for your peers.
3. Find greater health, fulfilment, and clarity.
4. Raise more mindful families.
5. Inspire positive change in communities.

If you find this helpful book, you are encouraged to serve as ambassadors for the Joyful Balance movement. Pass on what you have learned, coach your friends, and gift this book forward. This ripple effect of balanced living can create a culture of healthier, happier success in organizations and society.

You can drop me a mail at jbauthornash@gmail.com on what you found useful about this book, any other topics we might have to include in the next edition or any other feedback. I will do my best to read all emails and respond as appropriate. Thank you.

PART 5

NASH MEMOIR – PERSONAL JOURNEY

Chapter 15

JOYFUL BALANCE IN ACTION

My Personal Story

My story is about how redefining success and embracing joyful balance transformed my life. I went from being a burnt-out corporate leader obsessed with career growth to becoming a fulfilled individual living a holistic, purpose-driven life. This book is not just my story of transformation—it's an invitation for you to discover your own version of joyful balance.

Early life & Family

I come from a middle-class family in Chennai, where values, education, and resilience shaped my early years. My father, a journalist with a modest income, and my mother, the first woman in her family to graduate in 1953, instilled in us the importance of knowledge and perseverance. I grew up in a joint family on

Ranganathan Street, T. Nagar—now a bustling landmark named after my great-grandfather, a respected civil servant during the British Raj.

My grandfather, Dr. T. S. Raghavan, was a pioneering cytogeneticist who earned his Ph.D. in Botany from King's College, London, in the 1930s. His research on high-yielding varieties of rice, sugarcane, and coconut was instrumental to India's Green Revolution. My father, T. Govindarajan, was a sportswriter at The Hindu for 35 years and served as President of the Sports Journalists' Federation of India.

This legacy of achievement and service deeply influenced me. Today, I am blessed with my wife Priya—a software engineer and homemaker—and our two wonderful daughters, Deepthi and Preethi, who continue to bring joy and purpose to my life.

Education & Work experience

I completed my schooling at Madras Christian College School and, during that time, pursued my passion for tennis.

I subsequently studied Mechanical Engineering at PSG Tech, Coimbatore, followed by an MBA in Marketing and Finance from BIM, Trichy. My professional journey began in Indore, Madhya Pradesh, as an Area Sales Manager for Eicher Mitsubishi. Having come from Tamil Nadu with limited knowledge of Hindi, I had to quickly adapt and learn the language to succeed in my role.

Soon after, I moved to Muscat, Oman, where I worked as a Product Executive for Ford Cars and Trucks with one of West Asia's largest Ford distributors. Five years in the automotive industry provided valuable grounding, but in 1996, I entered the burgeoning IT sector by joining a joint venture between HCL and HP in India.

In 1997, through the DEC/Compaq acquisition, I joined Hewlett-Packard and spent the next 25 years building a diverse career across Category and Channel Management, Services, Marketing, and E-commerce in India and Asia-Pacific Japan. In 2022, I was appointed Services Business Leader for HP Online Store across EMEA (Europe, Middle East & Africa) and APJ (Asia Pacific & Japan)—marking a proud milestone in my 25-year journey with HP.

My unique full name

My parents named me Narasimhan, after the Man-Lion avatar of Lord Vishnu. The surname Tupil traces its origins to Sri Vedanta Desika, a revered Hindu Guru from the village of Thoopul (Tupil) near the ancient city of Kanchipuram in Tamil Nadu.

The name Nash came much later, in 1993, when I was working in Oman for a major Ford distributor. My American colleague and Ford veteran, Theodore J. Battistone, struggled to pronounce my first name. With his characteristic politeness, he asked, "May I call you Nash?" I agreed, and the name stuck. Since then, friends and colleagues around the world know me simply as Nash.

Professional Rise & Burnout

I built a successful career at Hewlett-Packard (HP), achieving milestones at a rapid pace. By the time I turned 30, I was already a Country Manager for the PC Category. Before 40, I had become the CMO & Marketing Director for HP's large and profitable Technology Services business in Asia-Pacific. I was recognized as Top Talent at HP Inc. and was privileged to attend executive programs at IIM Bangalore, INSEAD Singapore, and ISB Hyderabad.

I wore my long work hours—50 to 60 a week—as a badge of honour. Within a decade, I had moved from being an individual contributor to a director managing managers, something I took pride in.

But this fast rise came at a high cost. Work began to overshadow everything else in my life. As APJ Marketing Head, I spent nearly half the month traveling extensive distances between Tokyo, Sydney, Beijing, Bangalore, and other major cities across China, India, Japan, the South Pacific, and Southeast Asia. The relentless travel, constant pressure, poor diet, lack of exercise, and little time for hobbies began to erode my health and happiness.

Eventually, I hit a wall. I was no longer giving my best to HP or to myself. I felt drained, uninspired, and burnt out. The career I once loved no longer brought me joy. That's when I knew I needed a pause. I took a break—and soon after, I decided to step away from HP.

Rising again, with joyfully balanced life

After my break, just as I was ready to quit HP, I was offered an opportunity to take up a smaller role in a different division—one that required little travel and allowed me to work at my own pace. It happened to be in an area I deeply enjoyed: E-commerce.

This became a turning point in my professional journey. From 2015 onward, I began approaching life with a more balanced and holistic perspective.

I recognized the importance of nurturing not only my career but also my well-being. I focused on financial independence, deepened my relationships with family and friends, and rediscovered hobbies and life skills that had been on hold for a long time. Adventure motorbiking, teaching E-commerce at a business school, volunteering for community service, pursuing photography—which earlier earned me recognition as an award-winning photographer—and writing prolifically as a blogger all became fulfilling parts of my life.

These diverse pursuits rekindled my curiosity, creativity, vitality, and optimism. Later, I learned that this way of living—blending multiple passions and hobbies—is known as a "Portfolio Life," a concept popularized by Christina Wallace of Harvard Business School. For me, it became not just a concept, but a way of living with purpose and joy.

Building the joyful balance and its benefits

The first step toward creating a joyful balance is to define your own success metrics—shaped by your Purpose, Passion, and Potential. Once these are clear, you can pursue them with Planning, People, and Persistence. In this book, I share lessons from my own mistakes as well as the triumphs that followed, so you can avoid the same pitfalls and accelerate your journey. My goal is to help you design a life where success and happiness go hand in hand—allowing you to thrive joyfully at work, in life, and beyond.

Benefits at work

Ironically, when I shifted my focus beyond work, my performance at work improved dramatically. The skills, energy, and perspective I gained from other areas of life began enriching my professional journey. Over the last decade in E-commerce, I helped grow HP India's online business 4x in just seven years and led the digital transformation of 600 retail stores across 300 cities. Along the way, I was humbled to receive the President's Club Award—HP's highest sales honour (2016), the Amaze Club Award from HP's CEO (2019), and the 25 Years of Service Award (2022).

In 2023, my alma mater, BIM Trichy, recognized me with its Distinguished Alumni Award, and White Page International, London, listed me among the Global Top 200 Marketers. What's most striking is that all these milestones came after I embraced a more balanced, holistic approach to life.

Benefits beyond work

Between 2021 and 2025—well into my 50s—I embraced some of the most challenging and fulfilling adventures of my life on two wheels. I rode through the icy Himalayan winters from Guwahati to Tawang near the China border, navigated the thin air of Ladakh to Umling La at 19,000 feet, and completed a solo 1,600 km journey across Tamil Nadu, ending at Kanyakumari, where three seas converge. I also explored Karnataka, Andhra

Pradesh, and Goa on several solo rides from Bangalore. Each trip tested my endurance, resilience, and spirit of exploration.

Parallel to this, I entered academia in 2021 as a Professor of Practice at BIM, Trichy, where I taught E-commerce to MBA students. Over the past four years, the course has consistently been among the most popular and highest-rated electives.

I've also had the privilege of mentoring and coaching hundreds of leaders, within and outside my organization, on topics ranging from Happiness & Success in Career to Customer Obsession, Digital and E-commerce Business, and Living the HP Way.

Since adapting the Portfolio Life approach a decade ago, I've written more than 100 articles on subjects close to my heart—Indian culture, sports, leadership, travel, and motorbiking. Writing, along with adventure motorbiking, university teaching, and leadership coaching, has become my set of "flow state" activities—where I feel intensely focused, energized, and joyful.

Ironically, it is these pursuits outside work that have made me a far stronger professional inside work. They align with my natural strengths and passions, and most importantly, they make me happy. I often encourage people to carve out their own authentic path—recognizing that a career is only one part of life. When your work and hobbies align with your purpose, passion, and potential, success inevitably follows.

This book is dedicated to my beloved wife, Padmapriya—known to most as Priya—who has stood by me through thick and thin for nearly three decades. She is my true-life partner in every sense of the word. Her love, patience, kindness, sense of duty, and quiet maturity have been a constant source of inspiration. She has always encouraged me to live a balanced life, and because of her, I am a happier and better person. Together, we have built a joyful family and raised two wonderful daughters, Deepthi and Preethi, who continue to be our pride and delight.

Chapter 16

LIFE LEARNINGS AS TEACHER, VOLUNTEER, MOTORCYCLIST, PHOTOGRAPHER, SINGER AND WRITER

"In life and art, it's better to be an enthusiastic amateur than a jaded professional."

– Robert Genn

"Practice any art, music, singing, dancing, acting, drawing, painting, sculpting, poetry, fiction, essays, reportage, no matter how well or badly, not to get money and fame, but to experience becoming, to find out what's inside you, to make your soul grow."

– Kurt Vonnegut, American author, satirist, and graphic artist

I am not a professional teacher or biker or photographer or singer. I prefer to call myself, proudly a "High class amateur". The word "amateur" comes from the French/Latin root meaning "to love" (amator), focusing on doing work for the love of it. Amateurs are often seen as preserving passion, while professionals risk becoming jaded. And when you are willing to experiment, sky is the limit. These activities help the SOUL grow to be happy.

Learnings as a teacher

"If people remember me as a good teacher, rather than as the President or the Missile Man, which will be the greatest honour for me," - Former Indian President, Dr. A. P. J. Abdul Kalam.

I have been teaching E-commerce at BIM, Trichy Business School, for over 4 years now as a visiting professor of practice.

My learnings as a teacher:

1) To teach is to learn twice. Teaching others vastly improves our understanding of the subject. Although I am a professor of practice with over 10 years of experience in E-commerce, this field is rapidly evolving. Being a teacher makes me learn about new concepts every day.
2) Joy of giving back by sharing Knowledge: A key aspect of the job is inspiring and mentoring students, which can be deeply gratifying.
3) Creative Control: I had the freedom to design my own courses, lectures, and assignments within the curriculum. And tailored

it to be one of the most practical courses in E-commerce that any MBA School can offer in India.

4) Stimulating Environment: As a teacher, I am surrounded by intellectually curious students, creating a dynamic, engaging atmosphere. Connecting with the next generation. It's fun.
5) Professional Esteem: Teaching at a university is a respected profession. The opportunities to work with and learn from other professors, visitors, and experts foster valuable professional relationships.

Let me explain more. "Teaching is a very noble profession that shapes the character, calibre, and future of an individual," said our respected former President, Dr. A. P. J. Abdul Kalam.

His words deeply resonate with me. Most of us may forget the powerful CEOs or political leaders of yesterday, but we always remember the great teachers who shaped us—sometimes even decades later. As the saying goes, it takes a village to raise a child. No matter how big or small, we all have a responsibility to give back to our families, schools, colleges, organizations, and communities that helped raise us.

For me, teaching became that form of giving back. I never set out to be a teacher—it happened almost by accident. At an alumni meet in 2020, my B-School Director, Dr. Asit Barma, casually suggested that industry alumni consider teaching. That simple spark planted the seed.

With the support of my alma mater, BIM Trichy, I designed and delivered a full-credit university course on E-Commerce and Digital Business. Since 2021, I've taught this course as a Professor of Practice. Over four years, I've conducted 20 sessions annually, covering key aspects of e-commerce, and student feedback has been consistently encouraging, improving each year.

I deliver 20 sessions covering the following E-commerce topics.

1. Rise of the Digital Era, Digital building blocks, Omnichannel models
2. How India shops online, B2B, B2G, B2C ECom
3. ECom P&L, Financials ratios, category mgmt., web, call center
4. ECom, HR, Change management.
5. ECom IT infrastructure, security, privacy, GDPR
6. Online Branding, Social, PR, Digital marketing, Merchandising
7. Operations, Logistics, Supply Chain, Payments
8. CRM, customer service, LTV, NPS, TCE
9. Quick commerce, Fast fashion, Hyper-Value commerce, and influencer-led e-commerce.
10. E-shopping trends in Beauty, Electronics, Health & wellness
11. What to learn from startups.

I would like to express my heartfelt gratitude to the people who make it possible for me to teach year after year:

- Senior leaders at HP Inc. – for supporting my volunteering efforts to teach and share my 12+ years of e-commerce experience with students. HP itself has a proud tradition of industry–academia collaboration—after all, Bill Hewlett and Dave Packard were Stanford students encouraged by their professor, Fred Terman, to start what eventually became HP.

- My former colleagues at HP India's E-commerce team – across category and business management, digital marketing, online merchandising, call center operations, supply chain, and logistics. The knowledge I gained from working alongside them forms the backbone of many classroom discussions.
- At BIM Trichy, my sincere thanks to Director Dr. Asit K. Barma and Professor Ruma Agnes, Area Chair of Digital Business, for continuously encouraging and supporting my teaching journey.
- My students, past and present – every year, the number of students opting for the e-commerce elective continues to grow. Today, more than two-thirds of the MBA class (80+ out of 120 students) choose this course, making it one of the most popular electives at BIM. Their enthusiasm and curiosity continually inspire me.

As a working professional, I devote nearly 100 hours each year—on weekends and holidays—to teaching. It isn't easy to carve out time to prepare lessons, conduct classes, design question papers, create assignments, and then evaluate submissions for 80+ students, all in line with university norms. Yet I continue to prioritize teaching for several important reasons.

First, to teach is to learn twice—and in the dynamic world of e-commerce, teaching keeps me constantly up to date on new trends and ideas. Second, teaching is deeply fulfilling; it allows me to give back to society in a meaningful way. None of us would be where we are in the IT industry without the teachers and mentors who guided us.

For me, this is more than just a course—it is a shining example of how industry and academia can collaborate to shape and develop the next generation of business leaders.

Learnings as a community service volunteer

"Hands that serve is holier than lips that pray" is attributed to Sathya Sai Baba.

I would encourage everyone to do some form of community service. I volunteer in the community as a Sathya Sai Seva volunteer. Let me explain the insights and benefits of serving as a community service volunteer. As a Narayana Seva volunteer, I play a small part in distribution and serve home-cooked meals to poor, needy, physically challenged, and homeless people on the streets every week.

Benefits for self:

- Increased patience, empathy, and sensitivity to fellow human beings
- Improves sense of purpose in life.
- Improves our gratitude for all the blessings in our lives and the opportunity to serve others.
- Improved soft skills like planning, leadership, communication, and teamwork (for Example, in preparing meals, packing them, and distributing them to the poor and needy)

- Volunteering improves your mood and can significantly reduce stress, anger, and anxiety.
- Helping others can bring happiness, combat depression, and lead to higher life satisfaction.
- Fostering new friendships & Social connections by meeting new people from diverse backgrounds.

Benefits for Communities

- Volunteering unites people from different backgrounds, fostering a stronger sense of unity and connection.
- Service activities help to reduce loneliness and increase happiness.
- Volunteers help poor families get access to better nutrition, health care, and social security.
- Community service makes the local area a more positive and desirable place for everyone.
- Community service encourages individuals to focus on the development of their own communities (self-help)

Please allow me to explain more about how I became a Sathya Sai Seva volunteer. The Sanskrit word SEVA translates to "selfless service". It can also refer to care, help, homage, or devotion, and its core meaning involves performing duties or actions for others with affection and without expecting any reward.

Sathya Sai Baba (1926–2011) was a revered Indian spiritual master, educator, and philanthropist who championed the principles of universal love, service, and the unity of all religions.

The Sri Sathya Sai International Organization SSSIO operates globally, with 1,969 Sathya Sai Centres in 120 countries, engaging in education, health care, and humanitarian aid.

In 1972, Sathya Sai Baba founded the Sri Sathya Sai Central Trust. Through this organization, Sathya Sai Baba established a network of free, general, and super-specialty hospitals, medical clinics, drinking water projects, educational institutions, ashrams, and auditoriums to benefit mankind.

The Government of India issued a ₹100 (Rupees Hundred) commemorative coin to mark the 'Birth Centenary of Bhagwan Sri Sathya Sai Baba. New York State and many Canadian cities proclaimed April 24th as Human Values Day in his honour.

I am truly inspired by both the Sarva Dharma (unity of religions) logo and the five human values logos of the SSSIO. See below my explanation.

Sarva Dharma logo	SSSIO logo
The Sarva Dharma logo was drawn by Sri Sathya Sai Baba to symbolize the unity of all faiths and the idea that all religions are different paths leading to the same divine truth. The emblem features symbols of major world religions, such as the Om symbol (Hinduism), the Dharma Wheel (Buddhism), the flames (Zoroastrianism), the crescent and star (Islam), and the Cross (Christianity), arranged around a central circle.	The logo of the Sri Sathya Sai International Organization SSSIO contains the five human values that form the foundation of Sri Sathya Sai Baba's teachings: Truth (Sathya), Righteousness (Dharma), Peace (Shanthi), Divine Love (Prema), and Non-violence (Ahimsa). Sathya Sai Baba's central message is encapsulated in the complete quote: "Love all. Serve all. Help ever. "Hurt never".

Before 2011, I never believed in Sathya Sai Baba. Always thought when there is God, why do we need Gurus or Spiritual masters as middlemen? And used to dismiss miracles performed both by Shirdi Sai Baba and Sathya Sai Baba as magic and unscientific. My engineering education and logical mind could not comprehend anything that was not scientifically proven. This was till October 2011.

In April 2011, Sathya Sai Baba passed away. The state of Andhra Pradesh, India, declared 4 days of state mourning. High-profile people, including Indian Prime Ministers (both AB Vajpayee and Manmohan Singh), Union ministers, governors, chief ministers, film stars, sportspersons, and industrialists, as well as the common folk from villages and towns of India, shared their condolences. Still, I was not impressed, dismissing him as the Guru of the rich and famous.

Two things changed my opinion in October 2011.

My brother, Ranga, a rationalist not easily swayed by Gods or Gurus, returned from a trip to Puttaparthi. And began extolling Sai Baba's philanthropic activities as a human being, not as a Guru. In the areas where India requires the most assistance. Education, Health care, Nutrition, Drinking water, Sanitation, Tolerance, etc. Sai Baba even brought drinking water to my hometown, Chennai, from the Krishna River in Andhra Pradesh, which many governments could not do.

My good friend and former HP colleague, Sai Chandrasekar, whom I admire both personally and professionally, discussed the work he is doing in villages and towns as a Sai seva volunteer and how it has changed people's lives.

As a business student, I got curious about leadership principles in action here. I was wondering how a single man, or any leader, could build so many educational institutions serving students, hospitals with specialist doctors serving, and nutrition centres providing food for hungry people, all at no cost. How is it possible for any leader to do this, too, on such a large scale?

Before this, I had only seen another great leader, Lee Kuan Yew, former PM of Singapore, transform a third-world nation of 4 million people in 20 years into a fully literate, healthy, peaceful, and prosperous country.

But what Sai Baba did was even more inspirational. He transformed perhaps 10 times as many people, without holding any official government position, by inspiring millions with moral authority to help their fellow human beings. With his simple LOVE ALL SERVE ALL mantra, he made both the givers and receivers gain abundant grace.

In October 2011, I participated in Narayana Seva for the first time. It's a service in which we prepare home-cooked food to feed people experiencing hunger on the streets every Sunday. These people are usually old or visually challenged or have lost their limbs, who are literally left to fend for themselves, uncared for by their own kith and kin on the streets. Sai Baba referred to these people as Narayana, or "God". Serving them is like serving God. Sai Baba said, "Hands that serve is holier than the lips that pray." Narayana seva provided the opportunity to serve God in human form on the streets. More details at: https://ssssoindia.org/narayana-seva/

It was life-changing for me. I realised how fortunate we are when we see hungry and homeless people who can't fend for themselves. India lacks social security, and there is no concept of Dole. Unless fellow citizens help them, no one will take care of them.

More than that, I admire the thousands of volunteers who prepare food, pack it, put it in cars, distribute it without any reminders, like precision clockwork, work after work, 52 weeks a year, come rain or shine. And these volunteers work with almost no recognition except for the inward pleasure of doing good to fellow human beings. No management school or professional MNC can produce such dedicated workers who are on a mission to make the planet better.

That sense of service is so strong that the activity continues even many years after the founder's demise. Maybe that's what organized religion is in Krishna, Buddha, Jesus Christ, or Prophet Mohammed. To serve other people altruistically is the foundation of any great religion.

As Swami Sai Baba says, "don't look at what service you did, look at what service did to you". Did it make you a better human being, more patient, more caring, more sensitive, more forgiving, more giving?

Sai volunteers span nationalities, religions, and educational levels. From Brazil to Japan, from America to Australia, from Buddhists to Christians, from Doctors to Sportsmen to Pop stars to ordinary folks on the street, anyone and everyone can be part of this movement.

I participate in Narayana seva for many weeks each year. The friends I have made among fellow volunteers, and the joy I feel when I see a smile on the face of a hungry Narayana being served home-cooked food, are priceless.

Such is the grace of Sai Baba, who can convert even non-believers and cynics like me into useful human beings and allow us to serve, showering us all with his infinite grace. On innumerable occasions, I have felt his protection and grace.

The giver gets. Love all, serve all. Om Sai Ram.

Learnings as a motorcyclist

"Four wheels move the body; two wheels move the soul" – Unknown motor biker.

Learnings as a Motorcyclist:

1) Treat uncertainty as an adventure. And every difficulty is an opportunity to explore.
2) Power of positive visualization. Think of what can go right.
3) Confront your fears to succeed.
4) Falling is ok. Rising after every fall is key.
5) Biker, Bike & Terrain are like self, company & market.
6) Don't overthink. Just do it.
7) Seek balance of planning & spontaneity.
8) Know when to lead from the front and when to let your team lead.

9) Preparation is key and make time to recharge.

Benefits of Being a Motorcyclist:

1) One of the most joyful, therapeutic, meditative, flow-like activities
2) The sense of bliss, memories, and achievement after a long ride has no parallel.
3) Improves both physical and mental well-being.
4) Reduces stress and boosts creativity.
5) Provides a sense of accomplishment and purpose.
6) Enhances the self and social meta-skills.
7) Keeps you passionate about the goodness of life.

"A man is a success if he gets up in the morning and goes to bed at night and in between does what he wants to do," said Bob Dylan. The words remind us that true success is not just about professional achievements but also about making time for what brings us joy.

In today's world of 50-hour workweeks, late-night calls, endless travel, and relentless demands, it's easy to lose sight of that balance. For me, the balance has always been found on two wheels. Motorcycling has been my space of freedom, reflection, and recharge.

Over the decades, I have ridden thousands of kilometres across India. I've conquered Umling-La, the world's highest motorable road at over 19,000 feet in Ladakh, reached the easternmost frontiers of Tawang and Darjeeling, ridden to the southern tip of Kanyakumari where three seas meet, and cruised west to Goa.

Closer home, I have explored the diverse terrains of Karnataka, Tamil Nadu, Kerala, and Goa.

Three journeys stand out as milestones and teachers. In 2021, I rode through the icy Himalayas from Guwahati to Tawang. In 2024, I undertook a 1,600-kilometer solo ride to Kanyakumari and back. In 2025, I pushed myself to ride in the high Himalayas under low-oxygen conditions. What makes them even more meaningful is that I undertook them all after turning fifty—proof that passion has no expiry date.

Motorcycling, I've realized, is more than travel. It sharpens reflexes, builds resilience, and teaches you to adapt to uncertainty—whether harsh weather, rough roads, or life's bigger challenges. Above all, it offers flow, mindfulness, and freedom.

The lesson is simple: Success is incomplete without joy. Pursuing your passion—whether riding, writing, or anything else—keeps you grounded, alive, and fulfilled.

Himalayas, Ladakh
(Northern most part of India)

Tawang, Arunachal Pradesh
(Easternmost part of India)

Bengaluru to Goa (Western part of India)

Indian Ocean, Kanyakumari
(Southernmost part of India)

I. Himalayan ride to Tawang:

I dislike three things—cold weather, dizzying heights, and broken roads. Which is exactly why I choose to confront them all at once: by riding into the icy Himalayas on a motorcycle at 17,000 feet.

Sometimes, the only way to grow is to face your biggest fears head-on—and win. The feeling afterward is indescribable.

In December 2021, I set out with two close friends on an expedition to Tawang, near the Indo-China border. Just three riders, three bikes, no backup vehicle—only protective gear, warm layers, and the determination to endure ten days of harsh Himalayan winter. On rides like these, anything can happen. And often, it does. You slip, you fall, sometimes you crash. You might even break a few bones. But the essence of adventure is this: you always get back up. Every single time.

Many people obsess over everything that could go wrong. I've learned to do the opposite. I focus only on what I want—to ride carefully, stay safe, enjoy the journey, and return home with great memories. And that's exactly how it unfolded. That's the power of positive visualization.

In the end, life, like motorcycling, isn't about waiting for the storm to pass. It's about learning to ride through the rain, the wind, and the uncertainty with courage, balance, and joy.

After the Tawang ride, I reflected and saw several similarities between Biking and Business:

Good bikers can handle 3 things well.

1. Biker, the person themselves (reflex, stamina, agility, fitness)
2. Bikes, their machines (any type, adventure to sports, when bike works, stops, slips, falls)
3. Terrain, their environment (snow, sand, rocks, mountains, valleys, good roads, no roads)

And good businesspeople can handle 3 things well.

1. Self (constant learning to stay relevant, being fit mentally and physically)
2. Company (Customers, Innovation, TCE, P&L)
3. Market (recession, war, good times, pandemic, etc)

II. Indian Ocean ride to Kanyakumari Cape Comorin:

On a different journey, after completing a solo trip of 1,600 km from Bangalore (Karnataka) to Kanyakumari (Cape Comorin in Tamil Nadu) and back via Tanjore & Madurai, I reflected on the experience. It reinforced the following management lessons:

1. Everything looks impossible until it's done. Don't overthink. Just do it.
   Can I do a solo 1600 km motorcycle ride? Can I wake up every day at 4.30am? Can I ride on a saddle for 8 hours a day? What will happen if something breaks down? Have I packed everything I need? Hundreds of questions. There is only one answer: stop thinking so much and just do it. Take life as it comes, as an adventure, and do the stuff first.
2. Seek the perfect balance between planning and spontaneity.
   We need to plan the route, book the rooms, and pack the necessary items in advance. But I had enough room for spontaneity and could accommodate deviations, like visiting my friend's place, which was not planned.
3. Know when to team up, when to go alone.
   This trip demanded that I go slow, absorb things at my own pace, shoot lots of pictures, and write a travelogue - so going with a team of bikers is ruled out. Also, I'm not here to win

any bike speed contests. If I don't get like-minded folks, I go alone, as I did.

4. Preparation is key. Read about the places before you go.
   The story, history, geography, cultural and religious significance, etc. You will then see the temple or stone sculptures in a different light. Same about preparing for the ride, with everything from sunscreen, goggles, and protective gear to hydration and route maps.
5. Make time to recharge.
   I love photography, writing, motorcycle biking, history, culture, etc. Glad I did these now, as we are not getting younger by the day. The time-energy-money triangle must be ideal for enjoying things in life. Every time I finish a long bike ride, I don't get tired. On the contrary, I feel energized and return to the office with fresher ideas and more energy for office work.

III. High altitude ride to Umling-La at 19,000 feet in Ladakh:

This ride was special because I was already over 55.

1. This was the Highest altitude I have ever reached on a Motorcycle (19,000 feet)
2. Lowest oxygen environment, which demanded a lot of stamina
3. One of the team members was less than half my age at 26 years :-)
4. Most complex route I have ridden so far, Tarmac, Off-road, Sand, Snow

5. Breathtaking scenery almost at every turn. Arid landscapes, snowcapped peaks, lush green valleys, golden sunsets, the bluest of skies, and lakes.
6. Unique flora and fauna of Ladakh - Poplar trees, Wild Yaks, Pashmina goats
7. Unique Buddhist culture. And some great Ladakhi food (Thukpa, Khambir)

These trips require lots of mental & physical preparation and fitness. I am glad I pushed myself to do this. And find a week, to accommodate this ride, to pursue my passion for Motorbiking, despite a busy schedule.

Learnings as a Photographer

"You don't take a photograph, you make it."

– Ansel Adams,
renowned photographer.

Why is photography important?

1) Self-Expression and Creativity: Like painting or any art, it provides a creative outlet and a way to express individual perspectives, allowing us to tell stories and share our unique view of the world.
2) Storytelling and Communication: A picture is worth 1,000 words. A single image can convey a complex idea, a

story, or a wealth of information more effectively, quickly, and emotionally than a lengthy written or verbal description. It helps you build bonds with your friends and relatives.

3) Enhances your observation skills, promotes mindfulness, and appreciation for fine details. Photographers pay close attention to our surroundings, seeing details and appreciating the world from different angles.
4) Joy and Stress Relief: Photography can be a relaxing and enjoyable hobby, helping to reduce stress by providing an opportunity to slow down, focus on the present, and connect with nature. And brings joy to others, like cooking. You don't need to know how to cook to comment on good food. Likewise, you don't need to be a photographer to enjoy a good photo.
5) Preserves personal memories, documents family history. Helps you capture and relive important moments, from family events to personal journeys, creating a tangible record for future generations. I have a picture of my grandfather studying for his PhD at King's College London, taken in 1935. He is gone, but his photo is a treasure.

See some of my recent landscape pictures can be seen here:

https://nashmotorbikerides.blogspot.com/2025/04/epic-landscapes.html

I bought my first SLR film camera—a Canon Rebel with interchangeable lenses—in early 1993 while working in Muscat. That moment ignited a passion that has enriched my life for over three decades. Completely self-taught, I learned photography the hard way. With film, every mistake cost money, and only a handful of shots from a roll of 36 would be worth keeping. Yet, I loved the process. Through persistence and thousands of attempts, my success rate steadily improved, and I began setting higher standards for myself. Photography books became my silent teachers, guiding me through the nuances of composition, lighting, and the art of capturing people, landscapes, and fleeting moments.

One of my most treasured memories is a portrait I took of my maternal grandmother, Lakshmi Patti, draped in her Kanchipuram silk and holding a cordless phone. She loved it, as did my family. When she passed away, that photograph became a cherished heirloom, framed in the homes of many relatives. My father, a sports journalist with a keen eye, also played an important role in shaping my journey. Though best known for his writing, he appreciated good photography and offered constructive feedback that kept me motivated.

Photography soon moved beyond being a hobby—it became a journey of patience, learning, and connection. In 1995, the British Council launched a national black-and-white competition, Cityscapes, encouraging participants to capture the soul of Indian cities. My father suggested Presidency College in Chennai, with its Indo-Saracenic architecture. While photographing, I noticed the statue of Dr. S. Radhakrishnan in front of the college. I captured him, the educator, with the grand edifice rising behind. My father, with his gift for words, captioned it "The Educator and the Edifice." Out of more than 2,000 entries, that photo won third prize nationally. It was displayed in Mumbai for a month alongside the top 20 entries—a proud moment in my journey. Soon after, I also won recognition from Fuji Film in India.

Those experiences taught me an enduring truth: photography is not about expensive equipment but about how you see the world. After that, I stopped chasing competitions and instead focused on capturing moments that brought joy to people around me.

When digital photography arrived, I bought my first DSLR in 2004 while in Singapore. Over the next two decades, I photographed landscapes, architecture, and people, archiving thousands of images. In 2025, I added a Sony Alpha to my collection, but over the past decade, my most reliable companion has been my Samsung Galaxy S series phone. Some of my best pictures have come from it, reaffirming that photography is about the eye, the moment, and the story—not the camera.

The universal lesson is this: a hobby like photography can do more than give you joy. It sharpens meta-skills—patience, observation, creativity, and empathy—that enrich both personal and professional life. Whether through photography or another pursuit, everyone should cultivate a hobby that brings them learning and fulfilment.

Learnings as a Singer

> *"God Respects Me When I Work, but God loves me when I sing."*
>
> **– Rabindranath Tagore (Nobel Laureate)**

Why is singing important?

1) Joyful activity: Even bathroom singers can vouch, singing is a joyful activity
2) Stress Relief: Singing can be a relaxing and enjoyable hobby, helping to reduce stress
3) Joy to others: if you prepare and sing well, you bring happiness to others
4) Lyrics can inspire: Powerful lyrics of songs, can inspire people.
5) Shared experiences: some songs, bring back happy, shared memories of your past with friends and relatives
6) Social connections: On popular platforms like SMULE, Star maker, you can connect with others for duet signing
7) Bonding: in most get togethers, Karaoke singing (when done well) becomes a way to bond and make connections

I love Karaoke singing. I have sung dozens of songs in Tamil and English. Occasionally I can stretch myself to sing in Hindi, Kannada and Telugu a bit.

I did a four language (Tamil, Hindi, Kannada and Telugu) 20 song Tribute to legendary SP Balasubrahmanyam, in 2020, just a week after his death due to after complications from COVID-19. Sent it to my classmates, many loved it. I sang 70 songs (only first stanza) continuously for 45 minutes, as a tribute to 7 top Tamil singers of last 70 years. I did a four language Karaoke medley on stage at a new year party attended by over 100 people.

My favourite singers and artists are below in no particular order.

Tamil film singers - SP Balu, Yesudas, Malaysia Vasu, TM Soundarajan, PB Sreenivas

Tamil Music composers – MS Viswanathan, Illayaraja, AR Rahman

Hindi film singers – Kishore Kumar, Mohd Rafi, Sonu Nigam

Hindi film composer – SD Burman

English singers – Elvis Presley, Frank Sinatra, Roy Orbison, Stevie Wonder, Lionel Ritchie, Phil Collins & Elton John.

Learnings as a writer

> *"Don't write because you want to say something, write because you have something to say"*
>
> **– Scott Fitzgerald**

Why is writing important?

1) Fosters critical thinking and learning. Writing encourages you to be curious and think critically by forcing individuals to analyse, evaluate, and synthesize information. Writing encourages questioning, research, and evaluation of information from various sources, leading to a deeper understanding of topics.
2) Encourages mindfulness and reflection. This is even more applicable when you are writing a memoir. While we all live our lives forward, writing allows us to connect the dots backward, leading to great insights.

3) Enhances clarity of communication. Writing allows for the coherent articulation of thoughts and ideas, leading to clearer and more precise communication. It enables individuals to convey complex information, share opinions, and build understanding more easily.
4) Promotes self-expression and creativity. Writing provides a platform for self-expression, allowing individuals to explore and uniquely communicate their thoughts, emotions, and experiences. It serves as a creative outlet, fostering innovation and challenging individuals to think beyond boundaries.
5) Builds relationships and empathy. Writing can help individuals build and maintain positive relationships with colleagues and clients. Clear and concise communication fosters understanding and respect, while constructive feedback and expressions of appreciation strengthen bonds.

Apart from photography, writing has been a passion that has stayed with me for years. For over five years, I've been running three blogs, each reflecting a facet of who I am. The first explores Indian culture—my love for history, ancient cities, temples, and traditions. The second focuses on leadership, drawing lessons from the world of sports to highlight resilience, teamwork, and strategy. The third is about motorbikes, where I share travelogues from my road journeys and occasional reviews. Writing for these blogs has never felt like work; it is my way of connecting with readers, even if they aren't sitting across from me. That sense of connection brings me deep satisfaction.

Indian culture: https://indian-culture-nash.blogspot.com/

Leadership: https://nashtupil.blogspot.com/

Motorbike rides: https://nashmotorbikerides.blogspot.com/

My love for writing is rooted in family influences. My father, T. Govindarajan—known as TG—was a distinguished sports journalist with The Hindu for 35 years (1952–1987). A founder and key contributor to The Sportstar magazine, he later became President of the Sports Journalists Federation of India (SJFI). Despite his many accolades, he always chose to introduce himself simply as a "Writer." His humility and dedication continue to inspire me.

Another powerful influence has been my uncle, T. L. Raghavan, or "Upe Uncle," a respected corporate executive in the sugar industry. With his wit, sharp memory, and satirical perspective on life, his writing remains fresh and engaging. Now close to 90, he still publishes a blog post nearly every week—an enduring example of consistency and creativity.

In many ways, this book is an extension of that legacy. Through it, I aim to give back, sharing my experiences and insights on career and life management with professionals striving for balance. The universal lesson is this: hobbies like writing or photography are more than pastimes. They nurture curiosity, resilience, and joy—anchors that keep us grounded, connected, and fulfilled.

Closing words for this section.

Respected and loved, former Indian Prime minister Atal Bihari Vajpayee, wrote poetry even after becoming a PM. A journalist questioned, how he is able to get time, to pursue his passion for poetry amidst a busy job of running a noisy democracy of a billion+ Indians? He apparently quipped, "You may become an ex-PM but never an ex-Poet" thereby highlighting while positional power is temporary, the creative and emotional soul of a poet is permanent and outlasts his PM tenure. Likewise, for me, being a Teacher, Volunteer, Biker, Photographer, Singer and Writer is not just a hobby. It's who I am, long after I stop working in my corporate career.

PART 6

NASH MEMOIR – PROFESSIONAL JOURNEY

Chapter 17

GULLY TO GLOBAL. MY CAREER TRIUMPHS, TRIBULATIONS & TEACHINGS

Gully to Global (G2G).

"Life is lived forward but understood backward"

– Danish philosopher Soren Kierkegaard.

My career journey from 1991 to 2025. This is about my career journey spanning over 30 years, from my first job in 1991 in an Indian state known for Its Gullies (Ravines) to my global role covering multiple continents. How one job led to another, and in some cases, the earlier job experience became the prerequisite for a new job. I had carefully preserved every business card, and looking back at them brings me fond memories. My career journey might not be as significant as that of global CEOs of large companies. However, the power of dreams and persistence to work towards it is common to all of us in shaping the future.

The early struggles and later triumphs give the reader complete context for the second part of the book, focused on my learnings.

1. G2G - The Hindi Heartland Experience (1991-92)

One of my dreams was to do a Global sales job covering multiple continents of Europe, the Middle East, Africa (EMEA), and Asia Pacific Japan (APJ) in a large MNC. By God's grace, in 2022, my dream came true with this global role. But my first job out of MBA school was a posting as an area sales manager in one of the largest but industrially least developed states (province) of Madhya Pradesh, India. And the state was famous for Gullies, or Ravines, in the Chambal Valley near Gwalior. Literally a Gully job.

Dec 4th, 1990, many decades ago, I was in my B-School, in my 2nd year of marketing and finance. I got the good news: I was selected for a job through the on-campus placement program at a prestigious automotive company. As a mechanical engineer, I have always wanted to work for an automotive company. A Joint venture between Mitsubishi Japan and Eicher Motors India (makers of trucks, buses, tractors, and the famous Royal Enfield Motorbikes).

I was posted in the heartland of India. Indore, Madhya Pradesh (MP). As assistant manager, marketing (Area sales manager) for undivided Madhya Pradesh, including Chhattisgarh, the largest state in India among the 30+ states then. I had to handle all dealers, both corporate and individual sales of Mitsubishi trucks and buses, in that large area. The only problem was that I did not know a word of Hindi, the language widely spoken in MP. And as a sales guy, all my MBA and engineering proved not so useful, unless I could converse in Hindi. I literally learnt Hindi in 60 days on the job, using a formula-based approach, memorizing 2 greetings - Hello and Thank you, 5 food items – Rice, Bread, Lentil, Veg, Water, 5 questions- what, where, when, why, how, and 10 numbers - 1 to 10. And "karunga" (will do) is used 100 times for every English word, such as check, phone, visit, pay, etc. "Pay karunga, check karunga" etc.

Somehow, I managed the territory, as sales manager, successfully for two years on the job, personally visiting over 30 out of 40 plus districts, in bus, train and taxi, selling to companies like Scindia school, Cadbury, Pepsi, MP Govt, beating fierce competition from Tata, Swaraj Mazda and DCM Toyota and making Eicher Mitsubishi market leader in MP. One of my customers, I later learned, was a very popular dacoit from Chambal Valley!! I sold a truck to a dacoit!

New location, new language, new people, new customers, new food habits, I learnt many new things in 2 years. Most importantly, the resilience to stay on the job despite the odds and deliver results as a sales guy. And I learnt Hindi.

Key learnings – Resilience to stick through and get the job done.

2. G2G - BAC Ford Muscat & HCL Noida experience (1993-96)

In May 1991, I was posted to Indore, MP. In the same month, our former Prime Minister, PM Rajiv-Gandhi, was assassinated by the Tamil Tigers (LTTE). There were rumours that the plotters of the crime were in Bangalore, and they escaped to Madhya Pradesh

(MP). Unaware of these larger developments, I had applied for a new passport in Bhopal. And given my Indore address. Then, as a travelling salesman, I started touring Madhya Pradesh.

The fun begins when the Police come home to Indore to conduct a routine police verification of my residence address for my passport. And I'm not at home. They ask my neighbours about me, "Are you aware of a Madarasi (slang for anyone from South India) staying in your neighbourhood and his whereabouts?" They are unaware of the context of police searches and assume the worst. They think the police are searching for Rajiv Gandhi's killers, and they start looking at me strangely when I come back home. I had to show my visiting card and convince them I had nothing to do with Rajiv Gandhi's killing 😉

After some time, I came across an advertisement for a "foreign country job" in the Sultanate of Oman with one of the largest automobile distribution companies in the Middle East—Bahwan Auto Centre (BAC), the leading distributor and retailer of Toyota and Ford vehicles. As an auto enthusiast with experience at Mitsubishi, I was selected as the Product Manager for the Ford brand. In September 1992, I boarded my first international flight from Mumbai to Muscat, officially becoming a non-resident Indian (NRI) for the first time.

Landing in a foreign land was a jolt to the senses. The locals spoke a new language, Arabic. There were unfamiliar customs, festivals like Ramzan, and infrastructure far more advanced than in India—better roads, modern vehicles, uninterrupted electricity, and even perks like free water, food, petrol, accommodation, and almost zero income tax. I had to learn to navigate and adapt to three very different groups, each with its own expectations and ways of life.

1) Americans in Detroit. As a Product manager, I need to forecast and plan for all car and truck models on a rolling 3-month basis for shipment.
2) Indian bosses and colleagues who were professionals - engineers, MBA, Chartered accountants, Lawyers, sales and marketing people, etc.
3) Customers, who were Omani Arabs.

In Muscat, I learnt how to look at India from outside India. Many things we take for granted in a democracy like India are not there in a monarchy like Oman. At the same time, I learnt a lot from the Omani people, living among them for almost 4 years. Omani people are quite polite, cultured, plural (they had temples and churches in a Muslim monarchy), and deeply respect talent (not just white-collar professionals like us, but also blue-collar technicians, plumbers, and labourers). And locals roll up their sleeves to work, unlike many other GCC states.

As a product manager, I can test cars. I can also build cars. I loved riding the 480bhp, V8 Ford Mustang for the first time in 1993. Then we built a special Lincoln Town Car extended limousine that even had a dining table, a bar inside the car, and bulletproof glass. My friend Anirudha Modak was the sales manager, and I was the product manager, who designed and sold these custom-built cars.

In 1996, after 4 years in Oman, I returned home and got a job at HCL-HP as a Product Manager for HP Printers, Scanners, and

Graphic Plotters. That was a big career switch, moving from the Automotive industry to the Information Technology industry. The transition from internal combustion engines to integrated chips was a change. But what was common was the product marketing, 4P (Product-Price-Place & Promotion) skill sets. I was pretty nervous about whether I could do a good job. But my boss was a great guy, took a punt on a rank outsider to the industry, and I did a decent job. Decent enough to get a promotion from product manager to senior manager. From Printers, I moved to become business manager for Toshiba Laptops in India in HCL Frontline.

Then, in 1997, came the next big break: I joined Digital Equipment Corporation DEC. DEC was the second-largest IT company in the world at the time, next only to IBM. DEC was an engineering giant, a vertically integrated enterprise computing company, which made everything in-house from Silicon (Alpha chip) to Software (VAX/ VMS), including memory, hard disk, printers, etc. We made everything from Unix systems to Servers, Storage, Networking, Personal computers, and even DEC Printers.

Imagine, in 6 years after my MBA in 1991, I moved from an area sales manager in a remote gully province of India to the national product manager for the PC business at DEC India. After learning two new languages, Hindi and Arabic, moving from Cars to Printers to computers, meeting a host of cultures and people.

Those six years, 1991 to 1997, were adventurous, and the learning was intense. I got married in 1996, and I remember that in one of the first few months after marriage, I was asking my new wife, who is an electronic engineer herself, to teach me at home, post-dinner, how chips, buses, memory, and hard disks work! Nothing can be romantic in that. Thanks, Priya Nash, for putting up!

Key learnings – Adaptability in transitioning from the automobile industry to the IT Industry. Transferable skills. Steep Learning curve.

3. G2G - The DIGITAL India Experience (1997)

Over three decades, my sales and marketing journey revolved around the "4 Cs." I began with Cars (Automobiles), moved to Computers (IT industry), then Cloud (on-demand services), and finally Commerce (e-Commerce and Digital).

It was a sunny, beautiful day in Bangalore on 7th April 1997 when I joined DEC—Digital Equipment Corporation as Product Manager for desktops and notebooks. For context, DEC was the world's second-largest IT company after IBM for over three decades and the pioneer that invented and dominated the mini-computer market.

DEC's PDP systems, powered by our own RISC chips like Alpha, our operating system VAX VMS, proprietary memory modules, hot-swappable hard disks, and networking solutions, formed the backbone of industrial revolutions across many countries. In India, institutions from Indian Railways and Tata Steel to Bajaj Auto, banks, and telecom companies relied on these fault-tolerant, highly reliable mini-computers.

DEC was a breeding ground for legends. In those days, the who's who of Indian IT were found either at IBM or Digital.

But in the late nineties, this company with such a great history was in decline, increasingly facing competition from companies like Compaq, which horizontalized the IT industry. Compaq made very few components for PCs or Servers. Chips and motherboards were from Intel or AMD, Software from Microsoft or Novell, memory from Hynix or Samsung, HDDs from Seagate WDD, Graphics cards from Nvidia, network cards from Intel or Cisco, etc. This is such a contrast to DEC, which made everything from Silicon Chips to Software. Compaq computers and servers built on open platforms were getting faster and cheaper and giving companies like Digital and IBM a run for their money.

Digital was a late entrant into the PC market. After giants like Apple, IBM, HP, Sony, Toshiba, Siemens, Fujitsu, NEC, Samsung, Compaq, Dell, Acer, and Gateway, Digital finally launched its own PCs. But while they arrived late, Digital PCs were high-quality, robust machines that enterprise customers loved. Unlike Apple, Sony, or Compaq, Digital didn't target the consumer market; instead, it competed fiercely in the enterprise space with IBM.

DEC India was looking for a PC Product Manager. Having done well managing the Toshiba notebook business at HCL, I was selected through my industry network.

The culture at Digital was a stark contrast to HCL. HCL thrived on aggressive, fast-paced marketing, like Compaq, while Digital emphasized technology and services. Here I was, in the PC division of a giant services and solutions company, largely left to my own devices.

I was fortunate to have a great mentor in my hiring manager, Kapil Jain, an IIT engineer and Wharton MBA, who encouraged my aggressive, fast-paced marketing approach. Together, we grew our market rank from No. 7 to No. 3 in just four quarters. By 1997, DEC had even beaten both HP and IBM in India's PC business for a quarter, ranking just behind Compaq—right before Compaq acquired DEC.

In 1998, just a year after joining DEC, Compaq announced that it was going to buy DEC. A colleague walked up to me and said it would be "Adapt and Go" in the merger. The merged company will adapt DEC's enterprise server, storage, and services products. And keep Compaq's PC products. Thereby implying DEC PC business (and its people) would be shut down. When I asked my boss, Kapil, what would happen, with a twinkle in the eye, he said, "So what, Nash, if we are going down, let's go down with our guns blazing" - implying just put the pedal to the metal and continue to be aggressive.

Then I perhaps made one of the biggest gambles of my life. After Compaq announced merger plans with DEC, and we were still competing as two brands, we ran an ad in the paper. We attacked companies like IBM, HP, and even Compaq, saying our products were better: faster speeds and feeds, better service, lower prices. HELL broke loose. Newspapers covered this. After all, we were the underdogs, and they liked the size of the fight in the underdog to challenge the market leader. My friends told me that, with this gamble, I either get fired (for attacking the company that is acquiring you) or get promoted for doing an exceptional job. Hence, Compaq has no option but to retain you. The latter happened.

Digital (DEC) taught a services-and-solutions-based approach to customers, the importance of engineering innovation, the power of networking with top-notch colleagues with whom I still stay in touch, and a strong employee work culture. And I survived the first major merger in my company.

Key learnings – Take calculated risks, take a solutions-oriented approach to customers, and emphasize engineering innovation.

4. G2G - The Compaq India PC Category management experience (1998-2000)

In April 1998, before I even turned 30, I became the country category manager for Compaq Business desktops, a business that accounted for almost 40% of the company's revenue. Compaq was the No. 1 PC brand both worldwide and in India. India was the fastest-growing major market for Compaq worldwide. And I was on cloud nine. But all was not hunky-dory for me in the new Company. New people, new culture, complete change in the scale of planning across product, channel, customer, financial, marketing, and business management.

In 1998, notebooks were very costly (exceeding 2.00L rupees), and desktops were around 70k INR with a display. Also, the concept of buying PCs for the home was not yet fully established. So, a commercial desktop was the default definition of a personal computer. And Compaq was the Global No. 1 PC player and the No. 1 in both commercial and consumer PCs. We still had about 20 top companies making PCs, including IBM, DEC, HP, Toshiba, Sony, NEC, Fujitsu, Siemens, Lenovo, Dell, GATEWAY, and ACER, as well as local heroes in every country like HCL, WIPRO, TONGFANG, SAMSUNG, LG, etc. In such a crowded market, Compaq was No.1 globally.

In India, HCL was still No. 1 in units, though Compaq was No. 1 in revenue. It was a very proud moment for all of us at Compaq India when, in Aug 1999, about 1.5 years after I took the job, Compaq became the No.1 commercial desktop player in the market, beating HCL (my erstwhile employer) by unit shipments. This was a very special moment in my life.

Imagine the odds. We had a 50% price premium over HCL on average selling price, we still did not have a factory in India, and we could not participate in many govt tenders which insisted on local manufacture, our presence in the market was under 6 years vs HCL which had a 20 years channel presence and reach...imagine overcoming all odds and beating HCL in units. Enterprise, SMB, distributor, and commercial reseller customers simply loved the COMPAQ brand. We were the first to introduce USB, DVD drives, proactive warranty, error-correcting memory, proactive insights software, wake-on-LAN, and many other innovations to the Indian market. Compaq was the Apple iPhone of the PC era. Most desirable, high-quality, high-spec, high-priced premium PC. And I was the brand manager of this business and the brand DESKPRO.

Commercial desktops accounted for almost 40% of the company's total revenue. And our MD would not submit a forecast to his APJ bosses without getting my and my boss's estimates of the month-end close. For almost 3 years, I ran this business as category manager. And the pressure was intense. I got my first grey hair at 31, and the number of grey hairs is still growing 😀. I remember a particular meeting in Houston where Compaq HQ category managers from around the world met. They had a world map and put a red pin in every country where Compaq was No. 1. When I came up on stage and put the red pin next to the India flag on the world map, the conference room roared with applause. And I still get goose bumps thinking about that achievement.

It has taken thousands of Compaq and Digital employees across sales, support, channel, operations, supply chain, and retail and reseller partners to make us No. 1 in the market. And we had a plethora of leaders who took this PC business to a totally different level, most notably a few of my ex-bosses: Som Mittal, Balu Doraiswamy, Kapil Jain, Ravi Swaminathan, Rajiv Srivastava - across the enterprise, SMB, and Consumer segments.

Compaq did many things right in India.

1. Innovative products
2. Widest range
3. Loyal channel partners
4. Aggressive marketing
5. Amazing sales team (enterprise, public sector, SMB, retail, ecommerce)
6. Factory in India. Amazing supply chain and operations team.
7. The first exclusive retail stores for PCs in India - Compaq World (now called HP World)
8. The first exclusive online store in India for PCs (Compaq Cooldukaan, now HP store)

After 12 quarters of running a high-revenue business, I was on the verge of burnout. I was working 12 to 15 hours a day. I left home at 8am and came back at 10pm, almost 3 times a week. Both my wife and mom were very concerned about my health. And my wife was carrying our first baby. I hardly had time for her. While professionally, I was conquering every mountain, personally, I wished I had a job that was less intense and more strategic.

And here comes an opportunity in the year 2000. Compaq wanted to open an online store in India and was looking for an e-business manager. I walked up to my boss and asked if I could take that role. E-commerce was a fast-developing area. They needed someone with category and sales experience, which I had.

But my boss was not ready to let me go. He literally told me I would be a "fool" to give up a prized category job and move into an unknown area of e-commerce, which was only a project plan on paper!! But I'm an adventure-loving guy and have always taken the less-travelled path. Stuck to my guns and insisted I get the e-commerce job. My boss thought it would be too risky to give me a job where I could be underutilized. So, he also made me run the SMB business as a separate segment from eCommerce. I was okay with him allowing me to do e-commerce. Was e-commerce worth taking that risk?

Key learnings – Revenue focus, marketing and finance skills, supply chain management skills, and ability to stay focused.

5. G2G - Compaq India ECom Experience (2000-01)

YEAR 2000. We survived the Y2K bug. No planes crashed in mid-air. No bank shutdown. Mainframes and minicomputers running archaic Cobol code were reprogrammed to differentiate between 1900 and 2000, and we survived. My wife Priya, a software engineer herself working at Wipro and serving clients such as utility companies in the UK, was part of these Y2K days. Thanks to "high quality and low cost" Indian engineers from SWITCH (Satyam-Mahindra, Wipro, Infosys, TCS, Cognizant, and HCL), the world was saved!!

There was another phenomenon that was taking over the world. The Dot.com phenomenon. The internet as a business model was taking over the world. From New York to New Delhi, from Beijing to Bangalore, every company, from a coffee shop to a bank, was setting up its own e-commerce site. Remember the "We are the DOT in the Dotcom" ad of Sun Microsystems? In this environment, companies in the IT industry also began setting up their ecommerce sites, especially in the USA, UK, Japan, and other developed markets.

But here, in 2000, in India, things were different - Imagine the odds of starting e-commerce in this country.

- A PC at $1,000 costs roughly a year's salary for an average Indian.
- PC penetration was less than 1% for a billion-plus population.
- Smartphones had not been invented yet.
- The cost of a good cell phone was above Rs. 50,000
- Cell phone calls cost Rs 17 per minute

- The average internet connection speed on a dial-up modem was 56 kbps.
- The average Desktop costs Rs. 50,000, and a notebook costs Rs. 1.50 Lakhs
- I have sold a 16MB (NOT GB) RAM upgrade for a Compaq PC at Rs. 16,000

The only e-commerce companies in India were online media companies like Rediff, Times, and SIFY, selling cakes and flowers for under Rs 1,000 ($20 then). How crazy (or cutting-edge) must you be to decide to launch an online store for PCs ONLY in India? Compaq was crazy! And how crazy must a person be to give up a prized category job and jump into an unknown online business GTM that was just a project plan on paper? Nash was crazy. All crazy forces conspired to launch India's first online store for PCs - the Compaq Cooldukaan (cool shop).

- The average selling price at the COMPAQ store was Rs. 60,000.
- We accepted Visa, Mastercard, Cheque, and Demand Draft.
- We had 5 people in the Yeshwantpur office conference room taking phone orders.
- Imagine our call centre in a small room.
- The website was run by a few engineers in our own office.
- And logistics was done by our own Compaq people.
- We had 50 products, SKUs on the online store, apart from Compaq desktops and laptops.
- Canon printers, MS Office, Creative Speakers, McAfee Anti-Virus, and APC UPS.

Full of energy and enthusiasm for a startup. A very young team of engineers and call centre agents, working almost round the clock. We went live in October 2000, after 8 months of building, testing, etc.

Cooldukaan - Golden transaction Oct 2000. We got the first Golden transaction, the first order from an NRI in Canada, gifting a PC to his mom in Punjab. He paid money via SWIFT code. And bought a PC for Rs. 70k. Our team exploded with delight. We are now testing our billing and logistics systems. My call centre agents were following up and talking to the customer, the aunt who had a landline in Punjab, assuring the PC her son's PC, which was ordered from Canada, will reach her in Bhatinda. And I told my team not to celebrate till we delivered the goods to customers. In 7 days, the PC reached Bhatinda. And we took the team to TGIF in Bangalore and had a celebratory dinner.

First time, any company in India handled a sale of such high value via ecommerce purely on the trust of the brand name Compaq. I started crying with joy when the lady wrote in an email that she loves the orange Color Compaq Presario PC with JBL speakers hanging on the side. It reminded her of her dog, which had big ears like our PC speakers. See the picture.

As the Indian market was well served by our retail and reseller partners, to avoid direct competition with our own channel partners, we focused all our marketing activities on non-resident Indian (NRI) Populations. We started advertising in Canada, the USA, Australia, Singapore, and Dubai, and in other clusters where we had a sizable Indian population, popularizing the concept of

PC gifting. Ka Ching. The sound of cash registers, happy online customers, and the sound of happy customers was great.

We had an unreasonable sales target, though. Our Asia Pacific boss, an Aussie named Paul Blinkhorn (and my boss, the aggressive Mr. RAVI S), wanted this business to become 5% of company revenue in year one. Even after 20 years, many companies, including IT and non-IT companies such as Titan Watches, which have a strong retail and reseller channel presence, have not achieved this 5% online sales threshold. But that did not matter. We were all drunk with enthusiasm for pioneering work in e-commerce in India.

We completed a year of e-commerce operations. We sold about 600 PCs online against a target of 5,000 PCs (Learning - never set Compensation based on sales quota for new business). My team, instead of feeling happy, felt sad that we could not meet the sales numbers and missed out on full salaries. But do you know what happened? By selling 600 Pcs at a unit price of Rs. 70k, we had beaten all other e-commerce companies in India. The Times of India recognized us as the largest online store in India in 2001, across all categories, just one year after our launch. Also, my boss, Ravi Swaminathan, received an award from his Asia Pacific boss for being the best country for e-commerce. We were second only to Japan in revenue. Much bigger than Australia, Singapore, etc.

So, Ravi told my team and me that we should feel proud of our e-commerce work and not worry about our non-quota performance. He got my team's salaries paid in full. This is what leadership is about. Pushing you hard. Light up the fire within. Stay with your team through thick and thin. The e-commerce team felt happy at last. Next comes the second major merger in my corporate life.

Key learnings – Startup skills, project management skills, feeling of a pioneer in a market.

6. G2G - HP India Direct Sales experience (2002-2003)

Have you been part of any merger? Tech merger? How big? Not many would have survived 4 MEGA tech mergers in the SAME company. DEC-Compaq, Compaq-HP, HP-EDS, HP+ -CSC-DXC, THEN PALM, ARUBA, EYP, 3PAR, POLYCOM, HYPERX, OMEN, AUTONOMY, and a DOZEN "small" mergers...Plus a massive split of a 110 billion company into two 55 billion companies. I have experienced (survived, to be precise) all of it, and here to tell the tale!!

Next came the second merger of my career. On September 4, 2001, HP announced its acquisition of Compaq. Just a week later, the world changed forever when two planes struck the Twin Towers in New York on September 11, 2001, in a devastating terrorist attack by Al Qaeda. Life and business would never be the same again.

To "protect" me during the merger, HP's top management, including HR, decided to move me to the safer notebook category and away from e-commerce. I was initially disappointed, but I understood their reasoning. HP didn't have a significant e-commerce presence in India at the time, and its core strength lay in servers, desktops, and printers, not notebooks.

Assigning me to mobile computing—overseeing notebooks and the legendary iPAQ Pocket PC—was a strategic move to ensure my survival in the new organization. And it worked.

After the merger with HP, I stepped away from mobile computing and returned to e-commerce. Surprisingly, even though HP didn't yet have a proper online store, it had a strong call center and a well-known "Dial-a-Cartridge" service. I was made responsible for all direct sales, including enterprise accounts handled via Inside Sales Representatives (ISRs).

In May 2002, I became Head of HP India Direct Sales, selling directly across all three customer segments—Enterprise, SMB (Small & Medium Business), and Consumer. My Customers and Product Portfolio ranged widely: from GE in Hyderabad, purchasing HP servers' worth crores as a Corporate Direct customer, to Lijjad Pappad in Bhopal, ordering desktops and printers as an SMB Direct customer, and even a college student in Mumbai, buying a Presario notebook or a Rs. 500 cartridges over the phone.

It was the ultimate job. I felt incredibly fortunate to work for HP. This tech giant sold everything from a ₹5 cartridge to a $5 billion outsourcing deal—the landmark contract with Merrill Lynch Bank of America. From small individual sales to massive enterprise deals, I experienced the full spectrum of the technology business.

This was the first time I got to work with another exceptional set of colleagues—from the HP side—after the Compaq merger. Many of them were stars, or rising stars, in the industry. My role literally swapped with Subin Joseph, a colleague I had known from my HCL days. He had been heading direct sales at HP, while I was managing the Notebook category at Compaq. Post-merger, he took over notebooks, and I moved to direct sales.

The most remarkable aspect of this merger was HP's "Adopt and Go" approach. We simply adapted the best practices from one company and left the rest behind. For instance, we took Compaq's PC and server business models, channel policies, customer management, and marketing approach. At the same time, for printing, storage, networking, and Unix, we followed HP's policies and operations.

HP excelled in finance, channel management, operations, and governance. In contrast, Compaq was stronger in marketing, end-customer sales, factories, and e-commerce. By blending the strengths of both companies, we built a new, more powerful organization.

It was a challenging merger—the largest in the tech industry at the time—. Still, after a few initial hiccups, we not only survived but thrived. And eventually, the red vs. blue rivalry faded, and everyone became purple blue 😉.

I was a PC guy till the merger with HP. Once we merged in 2002, I started learning a lot more about enterprise products like servers, storage, networking, and the whole world of Printers - Inkjet, LaserJet, Scanners, Plotters, DesignJet, etc. My learning curve and my teams were steep, as the call centre I ran had to answer all types of technical queries. Imagine this company with the power of DEC, Compaq, and HP all in one. Still, IBM was big in our industry and had its own PC business. And Dell was coming in a big way. Lenovo was just a Chinese company focused on the Chinese market.

The merger of Compaq and HP in 2002 quickly led to industry consolidation in the PC business. IBM sold its PC business to Lenovo. And later, Lenovo acquired many local heroes, including NEC's PC business, and became the biggest competitor to HP in the PC business to date. Dell accelerated their direct sales model big time. Apple, Sony, GATEWAY, HCL, Siemens, Samsung, ACER, Asus, Toshiba, and everyone who made PCs could not compete with the scale of these three companies. They became niche players. The PC industry eventually became a three horse race with Dell, HP, and Lenovo as the three big players.

And I was going to literally have the time of my life (which I didn't know then), selling even more complex products and moving to HP Services to sell cloud consulting services. Even I pinch myself, asking, 'How did all this happen?' Basically, I was adventurous (willing to explore, just like a true biker) and lucky.

Now, after 6 years in an Indian job, Asia Pacific was calling me. I had to relocate to Singapore.

Key learnings – adaptability to a new organization & culture, leading large teams, and people management skills.

7. G2G - APJ Finance & Channel Sales experience (2003-07)

May 2003. After seven years in India-focused roles, I had the opportunity to relocate to Singapore for an Asia Pacific & Japan

(APJ) position in the Finance team. I was appointed Pricing Strategy Manager for the PC business, a highly strategic role as an individual contributor, reporting directly to APJ CFO and VP Finance, Chander Kishore Madan.

Though the role was within finance, it was essentially a product marketing job. Chander was an exceptional boss who welcomed having a marketing professional embedded in a team of chartered accountants, finance analysts, and directors. Even as a sales guy, I quickly settled in. Chander would often introduce me as a "marketing guy in a finance suit"—and he was right.

Those two years in the finance organization taught me the critical importance of governance, diligence, forecasting, cost, and Opex management, and how finance serves as a business enabler, directing resources to growth areas. HP's strengths, in fact, flow from HR and culture, finance, sales, marketing, and operations, in that order.

I led the gross margin initiatives project, improving HP APJ profitability by roughly 0.3% through better attach rates, reduced bid volumes, pricing premiums, and channel and direct GTM (Go-to-Market) profitability initiatives—all for a multibillion-dollar business.

2004 marked a major turning point. IBM, the company that had essentially invented the business PC industry (while Apple dominated the consumer PC space), decided to exit the PC business and sold it to Lenovo in China. Overnight, our biggest competitor transformed from a global US MNC operating in over 200 countries into a Chinese company with deep roots in

China and global ambitions. Lenovo instantly became our No. 1 competitor worldwide, leveraging IBM's offices, factories, channels, and iconic brands like ThinkCentre and ThinkPad.

Being an adventure-seeking, action-oriented person, I volunteered to be part of the war room—the core team tasked with strategizing and executing both offensive plays in some markets and defensive manoeuvres in others. This was a crucial experience. I also joined the Solution Partner Organization (SPO), dual-reporting to the VP and the Head of SPO, Tian-Chong Ng. The SPO manages channel partners across HP.

Balancing the two roles, I delivered strong results. In HP APJ—Lenovo's home turf—we gained market share over six consecutive quarters. What could have been our biggest challenge turned into our greatest opportunity.

In 2005, I moved full-time into SPO, taking responsibility for PC partner business development across APJ. Beyond share gains against Lenovo, we improved partner profitability by increasing ASPs for products such as workstations, accessories, and remote compute solutions. For the first time, I had a sales quota in USD billions, and for 12 consecutive quarters, we exceeded the budget.

Those were exciting times, made even better by the guidance and mentorship of two exceptional managers: Chander and TC.

I gained invaluable Asia experience, travelling to China, Japan, Korea, Southeast Asia, and the South Pacific. Everywhere from Vietnam to New Zealand, I was lucky to experience via partner events. One is to read about a country. Another is to spend a few days meeting HP employees, partners, and customers in the market. That immersion gives valuable insights. If I have meetings on. Monday mornings, I land on a Sunday to visit the local market and museums. I'm a history buff and have seen most of the important monuments of countries and museums like the National Palace Museum in Taipei, the Te Papa Museum in Wellington, etc. One learns a lot and becomes wiser by travelling and meeting different people.

My family lived in Singapore for 4 years, and my kids went to school there. We enjoyed our stay. And living abroad is an invaluable experience. Many things we take for granted in one country are not so easy in another. For example, in India, I could hire a car and driver, a cook, a maid, and a gardener for almost a negligible fee. In Singapore, I did not even have a car. On the contrary, the public services in Singapore, the Buses, taxis, METRO, Electricity, water, broadband and police worked flawlessly. In the 4 years I lived there, there was never a power cut. My mom, with so much gold jewellery, used to walk alone in her saree at night without any fear of being mugged. You can't do that in any major city in India.

My office in Singapore moved from the PSA building in Alexandra Road to Depot Road and eventually to the HPAS building in Alexandra Road. 3 different offices in 4 years. The best part was that my house was almost the same distance from the 3 offices. It used to be a 30-minute walk one way. I walked every day for an hour, up and down, with my backpack, carrying my laptop and home-cooked food. I was so fit that I could swim for another 30 mins after my one-hour walk every day. Singapore, as a nation, is very fit. I had friends over 50 running a 42km marathon. Forget that my mom, Jaya Govindarajan, used to walk for 45 mins every day in the evening, and she was 70-plus then. In 2007, a chance conversation with a colleague from services made me think deeply about what I must do in the future.

Key learnings – multi-country management skills, living abroad with family, finance and channel management skills.

8. G2G - The shift from hardware to services business (2007-08)

2007. Facebook was just three years old. The tech landscape was dominated by large service companies—IBM, HP, DXC, Capgemini, CSC, Accenture—and rapidly growing Indian IT powerhouses such as Satyam, Mahindra Satyam, Wipro, Infosys, TCS, Cognizant, and HCL. In Asia, China led the hardware game with companies like Lenovo, while India was emerging as a software and services superpower.

Major global services and software firms had either their Eastern HQs or significant R&D centres in India. In fact, companies like IBM, Accenture, and Capgemini stopped publishing employee split numbers because their India workforce had outgrown their home-country workforce. Hiring Indians made perfect sense: they excelled in math, science, coding, and technology. India produces more STEM graduates than any other country, including the USA and China.

Indians had two additional advantages over equally capable Chinese engineers. First, they were highly fluent in English, often thinking directly in English. Second, growing up in a noisy, messy democracy with imperfect systems made them inherently creative, frugal, and innovative problem-solvers.

In the place I lived, the best engineers gravitated to software (Microsoft, Adobe, Oracle) or services companies, not hardware. The economics spoke for themselves: the gross margins and profits in software or services were roughly 10 times those of hardware. HP's PC business made around 4% operating profit, while Microsoft routinely made 40%. End of discussion.

I wanted to move into HP's services side—this was before HP acquired EDS and later CSC (which later became DXC). At the time, HP was No. 3 in services, just behind IBM and Accenture, with large delivery and development centres in India. After 15 years of selling tangible products, could I now sell intangible experiences and services? It was a challenge I relished, knowing it would be a huge learning opportunity.

A chance conversation with a friend in Singapore opened my eyes to an APJ Strategy and Planning role in the services organization. I applied, went through several interviews, and discovered that my lack of services experience was considered a strength—I brought fresh eyes. My prior Asia Pacific multi-country experience and pricing strategy background helped seal the deal.

I was fortunate to work under Som Mittal, a legend in the IT industry. Former Chairman of NASSCOM, IIT-Kharagpur, and IIM-A alumnus, India MD of Digital and later Compaq, Som had also led global services delivery at HP with 20,000 employees across three continents. As SVP of APJ Services, he made me his Chief of Staff and Strategy & Planning Lead.

The learning curve was steep as I transitioned from hardware to services. I was introduced to multi-year, multi-country revenue models, and learned that Consulting Services was the tip of the spear, bringing the full HP portfolio—servers, storage, networking, PCs, printers, software, and managed services—into play.

One highlight that stands out: we won a $5-billion deal with Bank of America and Merrill Lynch, the largest outsourcing contract of that year—and possibly the decade—bringing every HP product and service into play.

2008. The world was shaken by the collapse of Lehman Brothers, plunging the global economy into a recession. Amid the chaos, HP spotted an opportunity and acquired EDS (Electronic Data Systems), one of the top five services companies. The combined HP + EDS services revenue exceeded $30 billion, and HP was crossing the magical $100 billion mark. This marked a significant pivot—from a hardware- and product-centric company to a total solutions provider.

Just five years earlier, in 2003, IBM still made PCs, and HP was a distant third in services. By 2008, HP had become a dominant global player across PCs, printers, servers, and services, earning the nickname "the Walmart of the IT industry."

Yet, the EDS merger also brought uncertainty. The HP Services organization was split into Technology Services (TS) and Enterprise Services (ES), with EDS merged into HP's consulting and outsourced services. People like me, part of the HP Services org, had to hope we were absorbed into one of the new units. This was the third time I faced job uncertainty due to a merger—after Digital-Compaq, HP-Compaq, and now HP-EDS. Thankfully, each time I not only survived but was sometimes even promoted.

Whenever anxiety crept in, I remembered my mother's classic advice: "If your company cannot recognize your talent, hard work, and contribution with a new role, it is their loss, not yours. Just move on—you will find a great opportunity elsewhere." Her words—filled with blind faith in her son, and a touch of divine reassurance—stayed with me.

I was eventually placed as Head of Technology Services for HP India in 2008, returning to India after five years in APJ, but this time as a services leader, not a hardware guy. Before turning 40, I was managing a multimillion-dollar technology services business, one of HP India's most profitable units. For the first time, I was managing managers, many older and more experienced than I was. The team was incredibly talented—the best engineers in the industry—handling complex tech challenges across sectors, from stock exchanges, banks, and telecoms to steel mills and auto companies, as well as retail. The diversity of customers and IT solutions made the work immensely satisfying.

By 2009, yet another organizational shake-up arrived. I was asked to consider a role as APJ CMO for the technology business, leading marketing across six geographies—Japan, China, Korea, India, Southeast Asia, and the South Pacific. I accepted—on one condition: that I could operate out of Bangalore, which HP graciously agreed to.

Key learnings – Services business skills, adaptability to new culture post EDS merger, managing market uncertainty.

9. G2G - The APJ marketing experience (2009-14)

2009-2012

Perhaps everyone likes a fancy title. BUT not all titles are equally powerful. Which company and who carries it make a difference. To illustrate, the chairman in China is either Mao or Xi Jinping, the most powerful person. We also have a chairman of our condominium housing society. Same title, different effect. However, the fact is that titles have a powerful effect on others in Asian society. Denotes seniority and hopefully some gravitas.

November 2008. Just before turning 40, I became a director. I held the CXO title of Chief Marketing Officer, Technology Services, Asia Pacific & Japan (CMO TS APJ). I was now directly responsible for the marketing function of a multi-billion-dollar, highly profitable business and region.

Under my purview were six major markets: Japan, China, Korea, India, Southeast Asia, and the South Pacific. My team executed demand generation, customer and partner engagement, analyst relations, press, events, workshops, and seminars across 22 countries—the most populous and diverse region in the world. The role carried significant influence, opening doors for the services business to countless customers across APJ.

A little vanity checks crept in, and I reminded myself: Who earns the respect—the company, the job, or the person? I knew I was replaceable. But both HP and the role of marketing head would endure, which kept me grounded.

Humility was another lesson I observed daily. Extremely senior executives would introduce themselves modestly. A perfect example was my dotted-line boss, Hideo Ohta (Ohta-San), VP of a highly profitable Technology Services business in APJ, who would simply call himself "Services Manager Asia." There's a lot we can learn about humility from the Japanese.

My manager, Michelle Weiss, one of the finest executives HP has ever produced, was an American leader who lived by and instilled the values of trust, respect, diligence, and people leadership. I've written separately about Michelle on LinkedIn under the "Great Managers of HP" section.

My team was a true mélange of cultures and languages—Japanese, Korean, Chinese, Indian, Australian, and Southeast Asian. From the outset, I made up my mind: we would unite this scattered team across Asia to deliver exceptional value to both our business and our customers. Between 2008 and 2012, we executed over 1,000 customer events—almost one major event per week—along with hundreds of account-centric workshops, partner events, roadshows, and analyst and press meetings.

I recall one event in Beijing, focused on green data centres. The scheduled speaker from HP America fell ill, and my team asked whether we should cancel or postpone. I said, "Let's do it—I'll speak." With support from my Technology Services and Marketing colleagues, I delivered a full presentation on data center transformation in English, with slides and Chinese translation.

The session was well received, and for that day, I was dubbed a "data center expert." The show, as they say, must go on.

Though HP's eventual split occurred in 2015, by 2012, under new CEO Meg Whitman, the company was quietly and rapidly progressing toward two distinct entities—an enterprise company and a PC & Printing company. Technology Services was merged with our servers, storage, and networking business units to form the Enterprise Group.

2012 to 2014.

I was appointed APJ Marketing Director for SMB, Channel, and Alliances, overseeing an almost $8-billion business. At that time, even Indian giants like Wipro and Infosys were doing less global revenue than we were. The company had not yet split and was still generating over $100 billion in revenue, with channel partners excited to see HP grow stronger year after year.

I led the "Partner One" program for APJ, completing a major overhaul to ensure that partners who invested resources in HP and sold our value-driven solutions were rewarded with higher incentives. Interestingly, this was a principle I had applied back in 2005 as a PSG Channel BDM—growing partner profitability—but now in a far more complex enterprise business. In PCs, we competed with Dell, Lenovo, and Acer; in enterprise, our partner programs had to outperform everyone—from IBM, Dell, Cisco, EMC, and Oracle to the smallest network hardware makers and the largest services companies.

We executed some truly memorable partner events. One was at Madison Square Garden in New York, set in a boxing ring where legends like Iron Mike Tyson had battled. As a marketer, I had to figure out where speakers should stand—on all four sides? In Las Vegas, we hosted a massive event with over 5,000 partners. My personal favourites were the boutique experiences for select top partners: watching Roger Federer defeat Andy Murray at the Australian Open, experiencing the F1 Sepang circuit in Malaysia with cars whizzing by, or hosting an intimate gathering in a boathouse on a lake in Vietnam. Some partners even remarked that HP's partner events were the best in the IT industry.

Beyond the glitz, we delivered substantial business growth in the enterprise partner segment. We trained and certified partners on servers, storage, networking, data centres, and services. One particularly innovative initiative was "Network University", an event inside IIIT Bangalore, conceptualized by my friend Uday Raghunath Birje—bringing hands-on learning to partners in a creative, immersive environment.

6 years in marketing. I was traveling for almost 120 days in a year. Every other week, I'll be on a plane trip abroad. My passport ran out of pages, getting stamped in so many countries. My chartered accountant even joked that if I travelled for another 60 days, I wouldn't even have to pay income tax (if you stay abroad for 183 days in 365 days, you are technically non-resident). I was working almost 12 hours a day.

Obviously, this took a toll on both my physical and mental health. A breaking point came when, on one Monday morning, I suddenly felt like not going to work. I did not enjoy my work, and I told my wife, Priya, so. Priya has never heard me say this. We consulted a doctor, and he said I had all the symptoms of burnout and might fall into depression unless I drastically change my lifestyle. This was a wakeup call. I consulted my close friends and asked for advice on what to do. Some of them asked me to quit HP and join a nonprofit company. Others said, "I must look for a different job in a different BU at HP." Perhaps do what I love, even if it was not a "big job".

I decided to take a break and quit after the break. However, as luck would have it, I got another job inside HP. This was a "smaller" country job in an area I loved E-commerce in HP Printing and Personal Systems (PPS) group in 2015.

Key learnings – Higher order Marketing management skills, direct people management of 10 different nationalities from Japan, China, Korea, India, South-East Asia and South Pacific.

10. G2G - India Omnichannel and Ecommerce experience (2015-22)

When I transitioned from APJ Enterprise Channel Marketing to India PPS (Printing and Personal Systems) E-commerce Direct Sales, it was one of the most complex moves within HP—a true three-axis shift.

- First, the business unit changed: from Enterprise Group (servers, storage, networking, services) to PPS (printing and personal systems).
- Second, the geography changed: from Asia Pacific & Japan to country operations in India.
- Third, the functional role shifted: from Marketing to Sales, back to quota-carrying days.

Suddenly, my competitors changed dramatically—from IBM, Cisco, Oracle, Sun, and Accenture to Lenovo, Dell, Acer, Canon, and Epson. The only constant was that I was still within the same company when I took on the role in February 2015. Just nine months later, on November 1, 2015, HP split into Hewlett Packard Enterprise (HPE), where I would remain for several years, and HP Inc., the PC and Print company. I was thrilled to be back in the PC business and E-commerce, now proudly under the blue HP logo of HP Inc.

When I took over the India Ecommerce GM job in 2015, the world of eCommerce had changed completely from 2000, when we were seen as pioneers in the e-commerce market. The following were the major changes in the span of 15 years.

- The buying journey is now on a mobile phone.
- Data cost is dirt cheap.
- Video was king.
- The media was replaced with social media.
- E-tailers like Amazon have overtaken brand.com stores with price aggression and variety.
- It's Omnichannel. Customers hop from online to offline to online almost seamlessly.
- Prices and products across brands can be easily compared on dedicated portals.
- The AIDA cycle in marketing, Attention Interest Desire to Action, has shrunk from months to days.
- GAFA (Google, Amazon, Facebook & Apple) was in full action.

- Google (via search algorithm), Facebook, with its billion-plus user base, became a media company.
- Amazon, with the ability to take losses for 20 years in retail, was a deadly competitor.

In a market like India, e-tailers like Amazon and Flipkart have made significant contributions by improving warehousing, logistics, and last-mile delivery infrastructure through massive investments. Suddenly, Tawang (Northeast India) or Ladakh (North India) was not too far away to deliver shoes or groceries from Chennai or Bangalore in South India. Also, with Omnichannel models, companies started taking orders online and delivering locally via their physical stores. Of course, only companies like Croma, which own both online and offline, can do that. A pure e-tailer like Amazon, or a pure retailer like Pai or Vijay Sales, can't do this well.

HP (Compaq), which was a pioneer in e-commerce in 2000, was not a significant player in the space for the following reasons.

- Unlike Amazon, which took losses in Retail due to AWS, we need to make profits in Retail.
- We have channel partners, and we cannot compete aggressively directly with them.
- The sheer scale of a multi-brand, multicategory E-tailer comes with its own advantages.

As an HP Store, we adapted a strategy of selling through private corporate stores (behind a login) while also integrating our offline stores with online channels to create a seamless system. Although I didn't come from a traditional retail background, our India MD,

Sumeer Chandra, entrusted me with digitizing retail operations under a project we called Project Parivartan.

I built a dedicated team for retail modernization, hiring a technology expert, an analytics expert, and an omnichannel digital marketing expert. Together with our retail colleagues, we built a new omnichannel retail infrastructure in just one year, connecting 600 stores across 300 cities to our online platform.

This system ensured that any lead from any pin code in India was routed to the nearest store for sale and closure. For the first time in 20 years of physical store operations, we could track real-time performance of individual stores, allowing us to customize product offerings and fine-tune promotions based on sales response. We introduced coupons, offers, and instant discounts in stores while maintaining excellent on-ground service.

With this digital retail omnichannel model, our retail partners could compete with the Amazons of the world. HP gradually grew its market share in consumer retail to over 40%, leaving competitors far behind. While the brand's online store sales were constrained by pricing, the digital retail business took off like a rocket. I realized that my team's value lay in retail innovation, so I expanded it further by bringing in specialists in digital marketing, analytics, and technology innovation.

In 7 years, our online sales grew multi-fold. But even more impressive were the digital retail sales. I realised some partners were hesitant to jump into digitization. Personally, I spoke with many of them one-on-one and allayed their fears. Eventually, everyone came on board, and project Parivartan was a success. But what delighted me the most was the digital transformation that happened among our employees. I conducted over 16 sessions covering 1000+ people on "speak digital" for our senior managers in finance, operations, supply chain, marketing, consumer sales, commercial sales, and even HR. Simply showed them how digital can positively change every part of HP.

Functional leaders and my good friends on the Leadership team happily supported these initiatives. They encouraged their teams to use digital technologies to make life easier for our customers and partners. This had a cascading effect. Suddenly, archaic paper-based systems, like our internal employee purchase program, were completely digitized with the help of the Payroll, HR, Taxation, and Finance teams. Many other smaller examples are also there in their own area. From being an online store guy, I became the de facto Chief Digital Officer (CDO) for HP India, though I was not titled as such. I was so happy when many of my colleagues reached out to me for advice on process transformation issues across services, categories, bid desks, etc. Glad I was helping them improve the company's productivity through digital process transformations.

Running a 24×7 online store and overseeing sales, marketing, operations, web, and call center end-to-end felt very much like a startup experience. Our core team had just five people handling all functions, with the rest outsourced. It was an asset-light, highly scalable, agile, and profitable business, and I'm glad HP recognized its value.

I learned a lot—handling customer escalations on social media promptly, delivering goods during Covid lockdowns, and optimizing marketing spend while competing with giants like Amazon. I also had the privilege of hiring talented young digital experts from other industries into our e-commerce business, building the next generation of HP's digital capability.

Being part of the HP India leadership team for seven years was equally enriching. The sheer talent, energy, ideas, customer focus, sales and marketing aggression, supply chain resiliency, operational excellence, and financial governance required to run a multibillion-dollar business in a complex market like India, day-to-day, month-to-month, and over multiyear planning cycles, was awe-inspiring. Simply working alongside such teams was an honour.

By 2021, after six years in this role, I had accomplished many milestones, including digital retail transformation and building the next generation of talent. I was ready for a change. After consulting with a few leaders within HP, the advice was unanimous: after 10 years in APJ roles and 15 years in country roles, it was time to seek a global position. Having already spent a decade outside India, I preferred a global role that I could do from India.

As they say, the universe conspires when you plant a thought in your mind. In May 2022, my skip-level manager asked me to take a global role at HP Store as a BDM for Services. It was a thoughtful offer—they had clearly understood my likes and strengths even before extending it. I loved e-commerce and services, and it was global yet India-based. I accepted gladly and enthusiastically.

Key learnings – Scaling up revenue 4X skills, Digital transformation skills, higher order E-Commerce skills.

Teachings from My Triumphs and Tribulations

Looking back, a few lessons stand out clearly in my journey.

I've realized that *not getting what you want can sometimes be the best luck*. In 1990, I didn't get into Wipro. In 1996, I joined HCL instead. Those five years gave me invaluable exposure to India's Hindi heartland. Without that experience, I doubt I would have been offered the role of Country Manager at Compaq India later. Time and again, setbacks turned out to be stepping stones, making me stronger and better prepared.

Here are some truths I've discovered along the way:

1. Opportunities often come disguised. Mergers are usually feared for job losses, but for strong talent, they can open doors to bigger responsibilities and even promotions.
2. The universe supports clear intent. When you set a goal—even if you don't announce it aloud—the right people, events, and circumstances seem to conspire to make it happen.
3. Karma is real. I've witnessed autocratic leaders—powerful VPs—lose their positions, while humble, hardworking juniors steadily rose to become MDs and VPs. Consistent goodness pays off.
4. Never let a job define your life. A bad sales quarter can shake your work confidence, but it shouldn't dictate your happiness. The joy of riding a motorbike, chatting with friends, playing a guitar, painting, writing poetry, or petting a dog has nothing

to do with your sales targets. Those are the real anchors of balance in life.

I feel truly blessed to have friends from my college days who have stood by me over the years. They don't care whether I'm a CXO or an individual contributor—they value me simply for who I am. Their affection, support, and presence through both the highs and lows of life have been a constant source of strength. That, I believe, is one of the greatest blessings anyone can have.

Chapter 18

LEARNINGS FROM GURUS AND GUIDES WHO WALKED WITH ME

"Every man I meet is my superior in some way, and in that I learn from him"

– Ralph Waldo Emerson.

Role models are among the most powerful teachers in life. They inspire us, model values through actions, and provide blueprints for navigating challenges. Role models may come from history, family, mentors, or professional life, and their influence often lasts a lifetime.

In my own 30+ year career, ten of my two dozen managers stand out as true role models—all from HP, where I have proudly served for over 28 years. HP itself, shaped by its founders, Bill Hewlett and Dave Packard, is a legacy of innovation, integrity, and people-first leadership that influenced global icons such as Steve Jobs. The HP Way emphasized trust, respect, and responsibility, producing leaders who created more leaders.

From managers of diverse nationalities, I learned lessons no MBA could teach—how to lead with both head and heart. Their example has shaped much of who I am today. The managers appear in chronological order of my reporting relationships with them throughout my career.

Corporate lessons from managers

From ***Kapil Jain***, my manager (1997-99), as HP India Enterprise BU leader, I learnt:

1) **Success is mastering 3Cs** - Your Customer needs, your Company offerings, and your Cost to deliver the product. It has stood the test of time; in every role I have had since.
2) **Market share follows mind share**: He took the unknown PC brand of DIGITAL and made it the No. 2 MNC brand by successfully segmenting, targeting, and positioning to the right customer.
3) **Teamwork makes the dream work:** We got the India factory done in record time for Compaq. Involving engineering, supply chain, finance, product mgmt. To chip and software suppliers.

From ***Ravi Swaminathan***, my manager (2000-03), as HP India PC BU leader, I learnt:

4) **Think BIG:** Aggression in all forms from Strategy, Marketing, Sales, scale, reach, business/ channel plans he always went for big plans and the jugular of our competitors and made Compaq (later HP) the No.1 PC Brand.

5) **Execution is strategy:** His speed and scale of execution ensured we set up over tens of Compaq stores (HP worlds), made Compaq the No.1 online brand, signing up Shah Rukh Khan as brand ambassador
6) **Hire the best:** Choosing to focus on duplication in the coverage model, he paid Top Dollar for talent in marketing, supply chain, channel, retail, etc. Few tigers are better than many sheep.

From ***Chander Madan***, my manager (2003-04) as Asia Pac Finance leader, I learnt:

7) **Past cannot dictate future:** He came from a relatively humble background, steadily climbed up the ranks in HP from a financial analyst to an APJ CFO, with his hardworking nature, amiable personality, and business acumen
8) **Give back to society:** A great philanthropist creates jobs and improves the standard of living of people. Instead of acquiring more material goods, such as luxury cars and larger houses, he gave back to society by founding a company.
9) **Dream big, but act bigger:** After 2 decades in HP, he started eAgetutor, an English language teaching tech platform, and trained a million people for better English skills to improve their job prospects.

From ***Tian Chong Ng***, a Singaporean, my manager (2004-07), Asia Pac Channel leader, I learnt:

10) **Balance is key:** He could manage his HP work effortlessly. Run every day. Eat right. Stay fit. Be a dad to a family of five children. Serve his country admirably in the Army. Spend monthly time on social service.

11) **Grace under pressure:** He transformed the partner programs smoothly, raising mutual profitability for both HP and thousands of our partners, involving multiple BU stakeholders like servers, storage, networking, PC & Print, calmly

12) **Power of metaphors:** He once very smoothly chided a colleague who put in a lot of effort but did not show results, using a metaphor. Gave the message, and he gave a face too. Very diplomatic, very Asian.

From ***Som Mittal***, my manager (2007), as Asia Pacific Enterprise Services leader, I learnt:

13) **Caring for people:** He genuinely cared for his employees and believed in Management by Walking Around. Had lunch with new recruits and youngsters in his team.

14) **Business is numbers:** He could spot the weakness or strength of any country or division within HP APJ just by reading the numbers, like funnel size, receivables, productivity ratio, utilisation rates, etc

15) **Calling a spade a spade:** He could convey with a disarming smile, very uncomfortable truths plainly and directly

From ***Michelle Weiss***, an American, my manager (2008-12) as Global Marketing leader, I learnt:

16) **Trust and Respect:** Despite being an HP veteran, when it came to Asia, she gave me complete autonomy to. Sitting 10,000 miles away, she had great confidence in my leadership as an Asian, Marketer & Manager.

17) **Diversity is strength:** We were among the best performing marketing teams because of her focus on diversity, gender, culture, age, experience, etc.

18) **Gold and Silver:** She once explained, Silver is measurable things like your title, salary, car etc. Gold is not measurable like Love, Respect, morale, etc. She taught us to focus on Gold.

From ***Hideo Ohta***, a Japanese, my dotted line manager. (2008-10), As APJ Tech Services leader, I learnt:

19) **Humility:** He introduced himself simply as Technology Services manager for Asia. A very simple way for a veteran vice-president of a very profitable business to introduce himself.
20) **Silence is golden:** In many team meetings, where he could have the final say, I always saw him keep quiet and let his team members talk about their achievements. He spoke very little, but when he spoke, it mattered.
21) **Loyalty:** One company, HP, for all his working life. Fiercely loyal to his customers, partners, and employees.

From ***Rajiv Srivastava***, my dotted manager (2015-17), as HP India MD, I learnt:

22) **Simplifying the complex:** Clarity of thought, simplicity of communication, and speed in execution he brings, makes everyone believe nothing is impossible.
23) **Leadership:** He fused contrasting professional strengths, like Strategy & Execution, Sales & Operations, Country & Region, Direct & Channel, Managing & Leading, very well.
24) **Being human:** Old world values, personal humility, hard work, integrity, being a friend in need.

From ***Scott Basford***, an Australian, my manager (2015-19), as APJ E-commerce leader, I learnt:

25) **Sharing is caring:** He ensured every country manager's weekly qualitative reports were circulated, so we understand best practices of other Geos, built a sense of camaraderie, and joint accountability.
26) **Rule of Five mails:** If you exchange more than five mails on the same subject, stop writing and call the people to avoid misunderstandings and close the issue
27) **Be there, when it matters:** He was always available when I asked for his advice, despite his busy schedule.

From ***Ketan Patel***, my dotted manager (2020-22), as HP India MD, I learnt:

28) **Make a difference:** From India Channel days in 2005, to India PC Category to APJ PC Category to India MD to WW PS COO to WW President of Personal Systems, he delivered outstanding results and made a difference in each role.
29) **It's the goal, not the role:** Irrespective of his role, he was focussed on the goal, of profitable growth, product innovation, sales and marketing aggression, strategic thinking, employee, partner and customer satisfaction.
30) **Finding Magic in the details:** Whether in organizing product launch or an employee event, he took care of the smallest details in a beautiful way.

These 10 managers had minor flaws but were exemplary role models for the qualities I have modelled in my life. Each of us can find great role models around us if we look carefully and observe their good qualities and model them.

Chapter 19

TRIBUTE TO MY PARENTS

My book would be complete, only if I thank my parents, who were role models in their own ways. They gave me roots to stay grounded and wings to fly in the skies. I am happy to reproduce two tributes. A tribute to my mother, Jaya Govindarajan, on her 90th Birthday in 2023. A tribute to my father, T Govindarajan, on his first death anniversary in 1999.

Jaya Govindarajan

A mother's role in education and professional growth of a person is very important. I owe a lot to her. Here is a small tribute to my mom. My mom, Jaya Govindarajan, born 1933, who is 90+ is a great grand mom. She was the first female graduate in her family back in 1952, when India's literacy rate was under 20% and female literacy rate was even lower. She placed a high value on education and educated her three children my elder sister, my elder brother and myself very well.

I remember when I finished my engineering and got a campus job, I had got my MBA offer too. My dad was worried about funding my post-graduation, as he had retired from work and was running the house with his meagre savings. My mom weighed in and asked him to fund my MBA despite financial hardships. I would forever be grateful for her support. When I got my MBA BIM distinguished alumni award in 2023, the first person I showed the award was to my mom and thanked her. She is courageous, caring, diligent, and determined. I owe a lot of my personal and professional success to the values she taught by her example.

This simple woman, who brought me into this world, and my elder sister and brother. This smart woman, who taught me 3Rs "Reading Riting Rithmetic" and supported my MBA dreams after engineering. This caring woman, who brought up Three children well, and has Four grandchildren and Three-great grandchildren. This resourceful woman, who saved lot from what little my dad earned, and taught us the value of being frugal with money. This resilient woman, who battled so many storms in life and always emerged victorious like her name Jaya. This honest woman, who taught us the value of hard work, simplicity, truth, integrity and level-headedness. And the loving woman, who always cares for her children, through thick and thin, near or far, in thoughts and deeds.

I'm grateful to have won the genetic lottery of having this woman, this simple, smart, caring, resourceful, resilient, honest and loving woman as my mother. Love. Respect. Blessed to have her as my mom.

T. Govindarajan (1927-1988)

A noted British Sports Journalist once remarked "East of England, I never knew anyone who could write better English" That was after reading my dad's article titled "Birds of Paradise" on the legendary Brazilian footballer Garrincha. His name was T. Govindarajan, fondly called TG, by his friends and colleagues. He was a sports journalist who covered Football and Tennis for "The Hindu" a leading Indian Newspaper for almost 35 years till 1987. He played a big role, in establishing and later editing "Sportstar" a print-only, multi-sport weekly magazine in 1978. He was admired for his poetic flair and elegance in writing, whether he covered a professional match, profiled a sports person or wrote a travelogue. He was viewed as an artist deftly weaving a story around a match, delighting many a reader and never as a tedious reporter of events. Despite his carefree attitude and utter lack of ambition, he excelled in his profession and was elected for two terms, as the President of the Sport Journalists Federation of India (SJFI), a position he held till retirement with a lot of distinction. He contributed to improve the working conditions and renumeration for fellow journalists. The peer respect he had from fellow sports journalists in other papers like Times of India,

Indian Express, The Statesman across India, showed his level of professional excellence.

But what I liked more than his writing was the man himself. He was born in a family known more for their achievements than money. His father was one of the first Indians to get a Ph.D. in Botany from Kings College London back in the 1930's. His grandfather was the deputy collector of Madras, during British India times. My father was however least affected by his familial expectations. While it was fashionable for young men in those days to take up Law as a profession, my father scorned the idea. Much to the dismay of his father, he experimented with his graduate education as a student in different fields, two years in Chemical Engineering and later an Honours degree in Economics. He was a good student, but never excelled in it, like his father or grandfather. However, he was very versatile and multi-faceted. In college, he excelled in various sports including Cricket, he was a good singer and a guitarist, and he was so dashingly handsome, that he was selected as Mister Madras Christian College in early 50's.

Out of college without a professional degree, he was on the lookout for a job. He took up a job as a sports reporter in "The Hindu" newspaper to pass time. His superiors liked his attitude to life and the style of his writing. And my father enjoyed what he was doing and he was happy about getting paid for it. That is when he stumbled upon his vocation as a writer and an employer, The Hindu, he never left for the next 35 years.

He had a modest income as a journalist but lived like a King. He had no professional ambition, but he excelled in his field.

Being a journalist, he had a knack of having a good rapport with many famous sports people, ambassadors, businessmen and bureaucrats. But he also shared his heart out with the next-door grocer and milkman. Though he had contacts, he never misused them. His house was simple but was happy entertaining his Kith and Kin. He had scant regard for money or power. But had a high regard for human excellence, especially in sports, be it Don Bradman, Dhyan Chand, Roger Bannister, Nadia Comaneci, Pele, Mohammed Ali and Kapil Dev.

He was also a true Rasika (connoisseur) of fine poetry, music, art and food. His view was catholic and never parochial. He could enjoy both Homer's Iliad and Kamba's Ramayana, Keats and Kalidasa, Louis Armstrong and Bhimsen Joshi. He would recite verbatim for hours, passages from Shakespeare, Lincoln's Gettysburg speech and Tagore's Gitanjali. He could sing most of Frank Sinatra and Jim Reeves numbers, apart from Kishore Kumar and PB Srinivas ones. He could enthral a crowd playing the mouth organ or strumming a Guitar. He could appreciate both Rembrandt and Raja Ravi Varma. He would cry watching movies like "Citizen Kane" or "Karna". He enjoyed good food and would savour delicacies of any kind – whether it be Mexican, Manchurian or Madurai. He was a good cook himself, and he could make a mouthwatering "Stuffed Capsicum Sabzi" or a "Chettinattu Kottu Masala" in no time.

He was helpful to all his friends and relatives, whether it was using his contacts to get a prestigious school admission for his nephew, a better job for his friend, free tickets to cricket matches and cultural shows or simply being with them when they needed him.

Some of his favourite quotes:

- Being content is a blessing. Sometimes lack of ambition is good.
- It is better to have loved and lost, than not to have loved at all.
- Strike the right balance between the Mind and Heart. Finally let the Heart rule.
- On artistry: GR Viswanath's 47 runs delights more people than Gavaskar's 100.
- When he turned 70, I asked him "What is your greatest achievement till date?". He replied, "I have eaten till 70 my way and have not yet been eaten" A line full of deep meaning.

A few things I learnt from him, sometimes just by observation.

- People remember smallest acts of kindness better than grand intentions. When he died countless people narrated to me how he touched their lives. I remember during his funeral, as a street cart vendor, purchased a garland, many times her daily salary and patiently waited in the queue outside our house, to place it on his body. From the humble neighbourhood vegetable vendor to sports stars to CEOs he had friends who cried when he died.
- Professional & Personal Integrity. Clear conscience is the softest pillow. As a print journalist, in its glory days before TV and Internet, he could never be pressurised to write anything, other than what he feels on the subject.

- Being active. At 70 years he was riding a cycle, doing daily push-ups, walking a few kms, gardening, cooking, singing, driving a car and playing street cricket with neighbourhood boys' decades younger to him.
- Enjoy the present moment. He could watch the starry skies at night, or passing clouds in the afternoon, for hours without doing anything else and enjoy that. He used to say "Doing nothing and living the moment" is sometimes the best thing to do.
- Knowledge with imagination is rare. He can visualize, paint a picture, write in a few words or speak extempore on literally everything from cinema, sports, culture, jazz, music to history. You can spend hours listening to him. Perhaps that made him a great storyteller and sportswriter.
- Lastly, style with substance is eternal. He did everything with style, flair and passion. Writing, Speaking, singing like Elvis, playing the guitar, mouth organ, western dancing, driving a car, cooking, dressing, cricket batting, bowling and even satire and humour.

He was never rich. He had no fancy designations. He was not famous. He was not a success by any conventional measure of a capitalist society. He was just another face in the crowd like you and me. But he led a life of his own and enjoyed thoroughly what he was doing. His friends and family remember him as an artist with a brilliant mind, for his helpful nature and jovial heart. There can be only one TG. And he will always be remembered.

In both work and life, he showed how success is complete only with happiness. And happiness needs a purpose to be sustainable. And he was great role model Joyful Balance.

End of the Book.

PART 7

ABOUT THE AUTHOR, ACKNOWLEDGMENTS & FURTHER READS

ABOUT THE AUTHOR - NASH NARASIMHAN TUPIL

Nash Narasimhan Tupil is a certified leadership and happiness coach, mentor to senior executives, E-commerce teacher at a Business school, Writer, TEDx speaker and a successful multinational business executive. He has completed three Himalayan adventure motorbike rides, well above 50 years of age. Nash was rated a top photographer by British Council in India.

Nash has close to three decades work experience with Hewlett-Packard / HP Inc. He serves as the HP Store Services Business Leader for APJ & EMEA. Before this, from 2015 to 2022, he was India GM of HP Store and Digital GTM. His team grew the HP E-commerce business 4x in 7 years. They also built Omni-channel digital technology, analytics, and marketing platforms for 600+ HP World Retail stores in 300+ cities. In 2000, he set up India's first Online store for PCs (Compaq) and, by 2001, made it India's largest e-commerce site by revenue.

Nash is an engineer from PSG Tech, Coimbatore, and an MBA in Marketing & Finance from BIM, Trichy. He has completed executive leadership programs at INSEAD Singapore, IIM Bangalore, and the ISB, Hyderabad. He has over three decades of work experience. He joined HP in 1997 as a PC Product Manager and steadily rose through the ranks. 2008-2014, he was APJ CMO for the Technology Services business and later for the SMB & Channel business.

Nash has won several prestigious awards, including the HP President's Club Award for Sales Excellence and HP Amaze Club Award from HP CEO Dion Weisler. In 2023, he won the Global Top 200 Marketer (CMO) award from White Page International, London, UK, for his contributions to the field of marketing over 3 decades. He is a Distinguished alumnus of BIM Trichy. He is an internationally certified happiness and life coach from Meta Mind International (MMI), in partnership with HRD India and Kotler Impact. He has coached and mentored many executives on achieving a joyful balance between success and happiness in work and life.

He writes three blogs on Indian culture, Leadership, and Motorbike rides. He lives with his family in Bangalore. His work and life experiences, as well as his passion for giving back, make him uniquely qualified to author this book on Joyful Balance. He can be reached at jbauthornash@gmail.com. More on his blogs and leadership & happiness coaching at NashInspires.blogspot.com or NashInspires.com

Key awards for Nash

HP Amaze Club award from former
HP Inc Global CEO Dion Weisler

HP President's Club award. The top 1% of HP
Salespeople win this.

Posing with my wife Priya. With the BIM Trichy, Distinguished Alumni award.

HP Long service award from former HP India MD Rajiv Srivastava

Global Top 200 Marketer award from
White Page International, London, UK.

This award is special, as it honours marketing l
eaders across industries and continents.

TEDx Speaker, 2025

Receiving the international happiness and life coach certificate, from Avinash Ananda, Meta Mind International, HRD India & Kotler Impact

Teaching E-Commerce as Professor of Practice at BIM Trichy, Business School.

Riding the “Himalayan Bike” to Umling-La, Ladakh in Himalayas at 19,000 feet.

ACKNOWLEDGMENTS:

This book is dedicated to my lovely wife, Padmapriya (Priya). Priya has supported me through thick and thin for almost 3 decades. She is a great life partner, in the complete sense of the word. Her love, patience, kind heart, sense of duty, and maturity are quite inspiring. She encourages my balanced life approach and has made me a happier person. Our two lovely and loving daughters, Deepthi and Preethi, are the motivation for writing this book. Thank you, my family.

I would also like to acknowledge the people below, who inspire me every day, for writing this book.

My late father, T Govindarajan (TG), was a sports journalist at THE HINDU for 35 years. For his integrity, work ethics, professionalism, loyalty, zest for life, kindness even to strangers, style with substance, and power of writing.

My mother, Jaya Govindarajan. Her unconditional love and sacrifices in raising her family, her ability to stay calm despite the odds, her persistence, her independence, her frugal living, and her quiet dignity. Thank you, Amma.

My uncle, father's youngest brother, T L Raghavan, who keeps writing a blog every week, and published a book, even at the age of 90. He was successful executive in the sugar industry for four decades and a prominent Rotarian.

My ancestor and guru, Tupil Vedanta Desikar (1269-1369 CE), was a highly influential Hindu philosopher, thinker, writer, and poet who made lasting contributions to Indian thought and culture.

My spiritual teacher, Sri Sathya Sai Baba (1926-2011 CE), touched the lives of millions worldwide with his charitable work in health care, education, drinking water projects, and his message of love, peace, and selfless service.

My role model for business and personal leadership, Som Mittal, Ex-Chairman NASSCOM, former India CEO/MD of Wipro Infotech, DEC, Compaq and SVP APJ of HP Services business. He was kind enough to pen this book's foreword.

My friend for over 25 years, Rajiv Srivastava, Founder & CEO, Coreops.AI, and former India MD and APJ COO of HP Inc. For being a friend, guide, cheerleader, honest critic, and notable example for work-life success, happiness, and balance.

My friend, coach, and happiness guru, Avinash Ananda. I have used his, Meta Mind 6P framework in this book, to illustrate my life learnings. He can deliver life wisdom with delightful stories and humour. He believes "Giving is Living".

My collegemate and friend for over 35 years, GSS Srikanth, Former CEO, CSM Software (now SOLIZE India), for generating impressive illustrations and graphics for this book, including the beautiful cover page.

Few other friends, who gave critical feedback to the earlier versions of this book, including but not limited to Ganesh Krishnamurthy, Arun Kottolli, Ashok Krishna Rao, P Raghuraman and Tanmay Dubey.

FURTHER READS:

Like Warren Buffett, I believe, the best investment one can make is in oneself. I am an avid reader of self-help books for the past 3 decades. I have also attended several personality development courses most notably from Adam Khoo in Singapore and Avinash Ananda in India. The following books have shaped me and have applied several concepts in my life. They are great books for further reading.

1. Winning, by Jack Welch, former CEO of GE.
2. The 7 Habits of Highly Effective People, by Stephen Covey.
3. How to Win Friends and Influence People by Dale Carnegie.
4. The happiness advantage, by Shawn Achor.
5. Atomic Habits, by James Clear
6. The Four: The Hidden DNA of Amazon, Apple, Facebook, and Google, by Scott Galloway.
7. Rethinking Competitive Advantage: New Rules for the Digital Age, by Ram Charan.
8. Thiru Kural: Pearls of Inspiration, by M Rajaram, with a Foreword by President Abdul Kalam.